RUDOLF STEINER (1861–1925) called his spiritual philosophy 'anthroposophy', meaning 'wisdom of the human being'. As a highly developed seer, he based his work on direct knowledge and perception of spiritual dimensions. He initiated a modern and universal 'science of spirit', accessible to anyone willing to exercise clear and unprejudiced thinking.

From his spiritual investigations Steiner provided suggestions for the renewal of many activities, including education (both general and special), agriculture, medicine, economics, architecture, science, philosophy, religion and the arts. Today there are thousands of schools, clinics, farms and other organizations involved in practical work based on his principles. His many published works feature his research into the spiritual nature of the human being, the evolution of the world and humanity, and methods of personal development. Steiner wrote some 30 books and delivered over 6000 lectures across Europe. In 1924 he founded the General Anthroposophical Society, which today has branches throughout the world.

D1562578

THE ROSE CROSS MEDITATION

An Archetype of Human Development

RUDOLF STEINER

Selected and compiled by Christiane Haid

RUDOLF STEINER PRESS

Translated by Johanna Collis

Rudolf Steiner Press,
Hillside House, The Square
Forest Row, RH18 5ES

www.rudolfsteinerpress.com

Published by Rudolf Steiner Press 2016

Originally published in German under the title *Die Rosenkreuzmeditation* by
Futurum Verlag, Basel, in 2013

© Futurum Verlag 2013
This translation © Rudolf Steiner Press 2016

A catalogue record for this book is available from the British Library

Print book ISBN: 978 1 85584 528 2
Ebook ISBN: 978 1 85584 486 5

Cover by Morgan Creative
Typeset by DP Photosetting, Neath, West Glamorgan
Printed and bound by 4Edge Ltd., Essex

Contents

Introduction

The Rose Cross Meditation belongs among the pivotal picture-meditations of the anthroposophical schooling path. It is indeed the only meditation of which the content and pictorial structure are described as an example by Rudolf Steiner in every detail in his basic work *Occult Science—An Outline* (1910). He repeatedly called this meditation a 'symbol of human development'—for it demonstrates the transformation of the human being's instinctual urges, at work in the unconscious forces of the blood, into a configuration of the soul which is governed by the I. The plant, in its selfless surrender to the forces of the cosmos, here serves as the ideal image to which the student, via specific steps, becomes ever more akin in thought, feeling and will. To the plant, or more specifically the rose, is added a further element: the black cross which, in the way it points to the mystery of death and resurrection, provides a symbol of the higher development of the human I.

While the picture elements of the Rose Cross Meditation, the red roses and the black cross, belong to the sense-perceptible world of objects, their combination into the meaningful symbol of the Rose Cross is brought about solely by the student who thus creates an entirely new image. This then becomes the starting point for further steps along the meditative path.

Rudolf Steiner developed the build-up of pictures and symbolism over many years. The prolonged process of its creation (Chapters 1 and 2), together with its significant thematic environment, reaches from the Rosicrucian verse *Ex Deo nascimur* ... (Chapters 2 and 7) via numerous descriptions in lectures and connections with other pictorial meditations (Chapters 4, 6 and 7) right up to the verse mantras accompanying this picture-meditation (Chapter 5). The sequence of themes will be shown in the separate chapters and is here sketched briefly for clarification.

As early on as 1904 Rudolf Steiner spoke in general terms about his appreciation of Rosicrucian wisdom (4 November 1904, GA/CW 93); indeed, appreciation of Rosicrucianism can even be found expressed in his earliest writings. The methodical aspect of Rosicrucian schooling, as an initiation method appropriate for modern consciousness, came to the fore in his teachings over subsequent years which at that time still took place within the Theosophical Society. This schooling method, loosely linked as it is to the Rosicrucian tradition, has, as Rudolf Steiner describes it,[*] little in common with the understanding of Rosicrucianism generally accepted in his day.[†]

Rudolf Steiner spoke about the Rose Cross and its significance in connection with the works of Goethe from 1905 onwards, focusing especially on Goethe's concept of 'dying and becoming'. He also considered Goethe's poem *The Mysteries* in several lectures. This tells in poetic images of Brother Mark's pilgrimage as he follows wondrous paths

---

[*] See Chapter 2.

[†] See also Andreas Neider, *Anthroposophie und Rosenkreuzertum*, Dornach 2007.

leading to a portal displaying a rose-encircled cross. Goethe's poem, which remained a fragment, endows the symbol of the Rose Cross with a special mood (see Chapter 1).

This mood also pervades the dialogue between the Rosicrucian teacher and his pupil mentioned by Rudolf Steiner in several lectures. In a kind of paradigmatic tutoring situation this centres on a comparison between plant and human being.

The Rose Cross specific to anthroposophy appears for the first time in its characteristic form on the invitation to the International Congress of the European Federation of the Theosophical Society. The invitation to come to Munich was extended by the German Section, of which Rudolf Steiner was General Secretary at the time. The image of the Rose Cross is depicted against a bluish-green background, here with eight red roses encircling the two intersecting beams of a black cross. Rudolf Steiner explained in a letter that eight roses were intended for an exoteric context, whereas seven roses, with three above and four below the cross-beam, would represent the esoteric Rose Cross.[*]

The texts assembled here (extracts from lectures,[†] pivotal passages from *Occult Science*, notes of the esoteric lessons and examples from the abundance of mantric verses relating to

---

[*] See GA 264, p. 124.

[†] With regard to extracts from lectures and the esoteric lessons, one must remember that these are based on notes taken by members of the audience only some of whom were professional stenographers. Especially in the case of the esoteric lessons, the texts were mostly written down later from memory and cannot therefore be seen as authentic records. They nevertheless contain valuable hints so long as the reader remains aware of the situation in which they were written down.

the Rose Cross Meditation) can present only a limited view of the theme as a whole, focusing on the Rose Cross itself. It goes without saying that for an overall comprehension of what is described it is necessary to consult the texts in full. In this sense the present selection from the abundance of available material should be seen as an introduction to Rudolf Steiner's works in their entirety.

The texts collected here are arranged chronologically within the motif of each chapter. Readers for whom the subject matter is new might do well to begin by reading Chapter 3 in order initially to gain familiarity with the completed final version of the meditation. What needs to be taken into account here is that in the book *Occult Science* the meditation is preceded by an introductory consideration of the being of man and followed by a description of the human being in his interrelationship with earth and cosmos. If the reader has studied this work, he or she will have followed a specific path in thought and thus have been provided with the thinking prerequisites necessary for coming to grips with the demands made by the meditation both mentally and in connection with the will. The present collection can neither replace this didactic and methodical preparation nor of itself fulfil its purpose.

In the way I have arranged the various subjects and texts I have endeavoured to provide a sequence that can indicate the breadth of this pivotal anthroposophical theme. I hope interested readers may continue to delve further into this field both among the collected works of Rudolf Steiner and in relevant further literature.

Christiane Haid

1. Sources—Goethe's Fragment *The Mysteries* as a Point of Departure

Knowledge could only be attained at life's expense.[1] A legend will explain what those in the know thought about this. When Seth wanted to enter into Paradise once more, the Cherub with the fiery sword allowed him to pass. There he found that the Tree of Life and the Tree of Knowledge were entwined with one another. The Cherub permitted him to take three seeds from that intertwined tree. The tree depicts what the human being is to become and what the initiate has already attained. When Adam had died, Seth took the three seeds and placed them in Adam's mouth. Out of these grew a flaming bush in which three words were written: 'Ehjeh Asher Ehjeh'—'I am he who is, was and will be.' The legend tells further that Moses made his staff out of this. And later on, the portal of Solomon's Temple was built from the same wood. Then a piece of it fell into the pool of Bethesda, bestowing magical powers on it. And finally Christ's cross was made from it. It is an image portraying life dying and ending in death while having within it the strength to bring forth new life.

Here is a mighty symbol: life which has overcome death, wood from a seed out of Paradise. This is what the Rose Cross shows us: life perishing and rising again. So it was not without reason that the great poet Goethe said:

And so long you have not this,
This dying and becoming,

You'll be but a gloomy guest
On the dark earth turning.[2]

What a wonderful correlation between the Tree of Paradise, the wood of the cross and the life sprouting from it! The Christ Idea, the Holy Night,[*] is to represent for us the birth of the eternal human being into temporal life. Human beings must apply this to themselves today: 'The light shines in the darkness,' and gradually the darkness shall comprehend the light. All those souls in which the Holy Night generates the proper spark will feel within themselves what it is that the Holy Night brings to birth within them, namely the capacity that will become for them a force enabling them to see, to feel and to will how this saying is reversed and comes to mean: 'The light shines into the darkness,'[3] and little by little the darkness has come to comprehend the light.

First of all we hear that Goethe wants to show us the pilgrimage of one such human being, hinting that such a pilgrimage can lead to many a wrong track, that it is not easy to find the right path, and that one must have patience and dedication in order to reach the goal.[4] Those who possess these qualities will find the light they are seeking. Here are the introductory lines of the poem:[5]

A wondrous song is here prepared for many.
Hear it with joy! Tell all from far and near!
The way will lead you out o'er mount and valley:
Now is the view obscured, now wide and clear,

---

[*] This lecture was given during the period leading up to Christmas.

And if the path should glide into the bushes,
That you have gone astray you need not fear,
For by a persevering, patient climb
We shall draw near our goal, when it is time.

But no one will, despite profound reflection,
Unravel all the wonders hidden here:
Our mother earth brings forth so many flowers,
And many shall find something to revere;
Maybe that one will gloomily forsake us,
Another stays with gestures full of cheer:
For many wand'ring pilgrims flows the spring,
To each a different pleasure it will bring.

This is the situation in which we are placed. We are shown a pilgrim who, were we to ask him, would not be able to describe to us intellectually what we have just put forward as an esoteric Christian idea;[*] but he is a pilgrim in whose heart and soul these ideas are alive, but transformed into feelings. It is not easy to discover everything hidden within this poem entitled *The Mysteries*. Goethe described it as a process which takes place within a human being in whom the loftiest ideas, thoughts and notions are transformed into feelings and sensations. How does this transformation come about?

We are embodied many times, living through one incarnation after another. We learn many and various things as each provides numerous opportunities through which we accumulate new experiences. But it is not possible for us to carry every detail over from one incarnation into the next.

---

[*] See the Cologne lecture of 25 December 1907 (see Note 4).

When we are born again there is no need for every one of those previously learned features to be revived. If we have learned a great deal in one incarnation, and have then died and been born again, there is no need for all our ideas to come back to life. We live with the fruits of that former incarnation, for we then live with the fruits of what we have learned. Our sensations, our feelings are in tune with the knowledge gained in earlier incarnations.

We find an expression of something wondrous in this poem by Goethe. It introduces us to a human being who, in the simplest manner—as though 'out of the mouths of babes' rather than in the form of intellectual ideas—imparts to us the highest wisdom as the fruit of former knowledge. He has transformed that former knowledge into feelings and sensitivities and is thus called upon to guide others who are perhaps more bound up in their intellect. In a pilgrim of this stature, whose mature soul has transmuted much of the knowledge gained in former incarnations into direct feeling and sensitivity, we are presented with a pilgrim such as Brother Mark. As a member of a secret brotherhood he is sent on an important mission to another secret brotherhood.

He journeys through many a region and, being weary, arrives at a mountain where he finally follows a path to the summit. Every aspect of this poem is profoundly significant. Having reached the summit he espies a monastery in a nearby valley. This monastery is the abode of another brotherhood, the one to which he has been sent. Above the gateway to this monastery he sees something out of the ordinary. He sees the cross depicted in a special way, namely the cross entwined with roses! On seeing this he speaks words pregnant with meaning which can only be comprehended by those who know how very many times these words have been spoken in the secret brotherhood: 'Who has joined roses with the cross?' He sees three rays beaming from the centre of the cross as though from the sun. There is no need for him to call up before his soul the significance of this profound symbol. Within his soul, his mature soul, the sensitivity and feeling for the meaning is alive. His mature soul is familiar with all that lives in it.

What is the significance of this cross? He knows that it is many things including, among much else, the threefold lower nature of the human being: his physical body, his ether body and his astral body. Into this the I is born. The Rose Cross denotes the fourfold human being: in the cross the physical, the etheric and the astral human being, and in the roses the I. Why do the roses represent the I? In esoteric Christianity the roses were added to the cross because the Christ Principle was seen as a summons to raise the I, in so far as it was incarnated within the three bodies, to become an ever higher and more lofty I. In the Christ Principle was seen the power to raise up the I ever higher and higher.

The cross is the emblem of death in an entirely special sense. [...]

Die and then become; overcome what you have initially been granted in your three lower bodies. Slay it, not in order to lust after death but in order to purify what exists in those three bodies so that in your I you may gain the power to absorb ever greater perfection. When you slay what you have been given in your three lower bodies, the power of ever greater perfection will enter into you. Into his I, the Christian individual shall absorb, in the Christ Principle, the power of perfection right down into his blood. This power shall be at work right into the blood.

The blood is the expression of the I. In the red roses the esoteric Christian saw, in the blood and also in the I purified by the Christ Principle, that which leads the human being up to his higher self where it transforms the astral body into Spirit Self, the ether body into Life Spirit and the physical body into Spirit Man. This is how the Christ Principle meets us with profound symbolism in the threefold shining beam combined with the Rose Cross.

Above the throne of the Thirteenth, Brother Mark sees this symbol again: the cross entwined with roses, the sign which is both a symbol of the fourfold nature of the human being and also, in the red roses, of the purified blood or I-principle, the principle of the higher human being.[6] And then he sees, as a further symbol to the left and right of the throne of the Thirteenth, what is to be overcome by this sign. On the right he sees the fire-hued dragon: it is a representation of the human being's astral aspect.

In Christian esotericism it was known that the human soul can be surrendered to the three lower bodies. If it is thus surrendered, the lower aspects of life of those bodies will hold sway in the soul. In astral perception, this is expressed by the dragon. It is no mere symbol but indeed a very real sign. The dragon is an expression of what must initially be conquered. In the passions, in the forces of astral fire belonging to the physical human being, in this dragon, Christian esotericism—out of which spirit this poem was written and which spread across Europe—saw what humanity had received from the hot regions, from the south. From the south comes that part of the human being which is hotly passionate and oriented more towards his baser sensuality. And one sensed that in what flowed down in the cooler influences from the north lay the origin of the initial impulse to counter and overcome this.

The influence of the cooler north, the descent of the I into the threefold bodily nature, is depicted by an ancient symbol taken from the constellation of the Bear, expressed by a hand being thrust into a bear's jaws. In this way the lower nature of the human being, depicted in the fiery dragon, is overcome. What has been retained in the higher animal nature was depicted in the bear; and the I, having developed beyond the dragon nature, was profoundly depicted by the outstretched human hand in the bear's jaws. On either side of the Rose Cross there appears what it is that the Rose Cross must conquer. And it is the Rose Cross which challenges the human being to purify himself to ever higher degrees.

This poem does indeed depict for us most profoundly the principle of esoteric Christianity [...].

The most significant among the symbols and signs we possess, the one which has been recognized by all occultists in every age, is the human being as such.[7] The human being has been and always is spoken of as a microcosm, a small world. And rightly so, for those who gain an accurate and intimate knowledge of the human being will realize ever more clearly that in the human being we have in miniature everything, every part of all that surrounds us in nature. This may not be easy to understand at first, but if you think about it you will come to grasp what is meant, namely that in the human being we have a kind of extract, a compendium of nature, of all the substances and all the forces. If you take any plant and study its essential nature sufficiently profoundly you will find something, however small, of the same essential nature in the human organism. And if you take an animal you will always discover in it something of what the human organism has absorbed.

Of course in order to gain a proper understanding of this it will be necessary to consider the evolution of the world from an occult viewpoint. Thus, for example, the occultist knows that the human heart would not be as it is if there were no such creature as the lion in outer nature. Let us go back to an earlier time when no lions existed. Human beings did exist, for the human being is the oldest being, but his heart was then entirely different. There are interconnections every-where in nature, although they are not always immediately obvious. When in the far distant past the human being was developing his heart to become what it is today, the lion came into being. Both were formed by the same forces. It is as though you were to distil the essential being of the lion and, with divine craftsmanship, form it into the human heart.

You may be of the opinion that there is nothing lion-like in the human heart, but for the occultist there is. Don't forget that when something is placed into a context, into an organism, it becomes entirely different from what it is when it is not connected. Looked at conversely, one could also say that if you were able to extricate the essence of the heart and then set about constructing an entity which is consistent with it when it is not being determined by an organism, then you would have a lion. All the qualities of courage, of boldness or, as the occultist would say, of 'kingship' in the human being stem from the connection with the lion; and Plato, who was an initiate, saw the kingly soul as being located in the heart.

Paracelsus made use of a very beautiful simile regarding this connection between the human being and nature. He said: It is as though the individual creatures in nature are the letters while the human being is the word they spell. Out there lies the great world, the macrocosm; within us is the small world, the microcosm. Out there everything exists of itself while in the human being all is determined by a harmony with the other organs. This is one way of illustrating, through the human being, the evolution of our entire cosmos in so far as it is connected with us.

One depiction of this evolution of the human being in connection with the world to which he belongs is to be found in the seals which were displayed on the walls of the auditorium during our Munich Congress. Let us have a look at what they tell us!*

The first depicts a human being, clothed in a white garment, whose feet look metallic, like molten ore. A flaming sword projects from his mouth; his right hand is encircled by the signs relating to our own planet: Saturn, Sun, Moon, Mars, Mercury, Jupiter, Venus. Those who know the Apocalypse of John will remember that it contains a very similar description of this picture, for John was an initiate.

---

*This and the following six seals were painted by Clara Rettich based on designs by Rudolf Steiner. See *Rosicrucianism Renewed* (CW 284).

This seal depicts what might be termed the idea of the human being as a whole. We shall understand this when we remember certain ideas with which the older members present here are already familiar.

When we look back in human evolution we reach a time when the human being was still at a very rudimentary stage of his development. For instance he did not yet possess what you now bear on your shoulders: a head. A description of human beings in those times would sound somewhat grotesque. The head only developed stage by stage, and it will continue to develop. Human beings today possess organs which have, so to speak, reached their culmination so that in the future they will no longer be a part of the human body. And there are others that will undergo a transformation, for example the larynx which has a prodigious future still to come, namely in correlation with our heart.

Today the human larynx is only at the beginning of its evolution; it will one day become the spiritually transformed organ of reproduction. You can gain an idea of this mystery when you consider what the human being already accomplishes with his larynx. As I speak to you here, you can hear my words. Because this hall is filled with air in which certain vibrations are generated, my words are carried to your ears and to your soul. When I speak a word, for example 'world', waves travel through the air—they are embodiments of my words.

What human beings bring forth in this way today is termed a production in the mineral kingdom. The movements of the air are mineral movements; the human being affects his environment in a mineral-like way by using his larynx. But the time will come when he will ascend to working in a plantlike way; not only mineral-like but also plant-like vibrations will be brought forth by him. He will utter plants. And the next stage will come when he utters sensitive beings; and at the highest stage he will bring forth his own kind through his larynx. Now he only speaks the content of his soul by means of words, but the time will come when he utters himself. And just as the human being will in the future utter living beings, so was there a time in the past when his predecessors, the gods, were endowed with an organ which uttered all things that exist today. They uttered all human beings, all animals and everything else. All of you here are literally words uttered by the gods.

'In the beginning was the Word, and the Word was with God, and the Word was a God!' These are not philosophical words spoken in speculation. John was presenting an archetypal fact which must be understood quite literally.

At the end there will be the word, and creation is an actualization of the word; what the human being will bring forth in the future will be an actualization of what today is the word. By then, however, the human being will no longer be in possession of the physical form he has today; he will have progressed to that form which existed upon Saturn, the materiality of fire. And thus it comes about that the creative power at the outset of world evolution unites with our own power of creation at the end of world evolution.

The being who uttered all things into the world which now exist there, that being is the human being's great prototype. Into the universe that being uttered Saturn, Sun, Moon and Earth (in its two halves, Mars-Mercury), Jupiter and Venus. This is what is hinted at by the seven stars; they are the sign that shows the heights to which the human being can evolve. At its end the planet will consist of the materiality of fire; and the human being will be able to utter creatively in this materiality of fire. This is depicted in the fiery sword projecting from his mouth. All that exists will be fiery, hence the feet of molten ore. Wonderfully poignant is the meaning of evolution as depicted in this sign.

When we compare a present-day human being with an animal we find that the difference between them lies in the fact that the human being owns something which the animal does not own. The human being has an individual soul, the animal has a group-soul. An individual human being is in himself an entire animal species. All the lions together, for example, possess but a single soul. These group-egos are just like the human I, only they have not descended as far down as the physical world; they can only be found in the astral world. Here on the earth we see physical human beings each of whom bears within him his own I. In the astral world we encounter exactly the same beings, identical to ourselves but clothed not in a physical but rather in an astral mantle. We can converse with them just as we can with beings like ourselves—they are animal group-souls.

Human beings, too, in former ages, had a group-soul; only gradually did they evolve to their present state of self-dependence. Those group-souls lived originally in the astral world before eventually descending in order to live within the flesh. When we investigate those original human group-souls we discover four species from which the human being emerged. When comparing these four species with the group-souls of present-day animal species we find that it is possible to say that one of these four can be compared with the lion, another with the eagle, the third with the ox and the fourth with the human being of the distant past before the I had made its descent. In the four creatures of the Apocalypse, lion, eagle, ox and man, the second seal thus shows us an earlier stage of human evolution. However, so long as the earth exists, there will also be a group-soul of the higher revelation of man represented by the Lamb, the mystical Lamb, the sign of the Redeemer. This grouping of the five group-souls—the four of the human being around the fifth,

around that great group-soul still belonging to all human beings together—thus gives us the second picture.

Something else also comes towards us if we follow human evolution a very long way back, over many millions of years. We find that although the human being is physically present on the earth he is not yet capable of incorporating a human soul. That soul was still on the astral plane, and even further back we come to a time when it was present on the spiritual plane, in Devachan.

In the future it will rise again to this lofty stage, once it has purified itself on the earth. From the spiritual to the astral to the physical, and then upwards again to the spiritual: this is the long, long evolution of humanity. And yet it seems quite brief when compared with the period of development on Saturn and the other planets. Human beings then underwent not only physical transformations but also spiritual, astral and physical metamorphoses. To trace these one must proceed upwards into the spiritual worlds. That is where one will hear the music of the spheres, tones which surge throughout space. When human beings enter once again into that spiritual world they will be surrounded by this harmony of the spheres. In occult language it is known as the trumpetings of angels—hence the trumpets shown in the third picture. These revelations stem from the spiritual world, but they are only revealed to human beings when they travel ever further. That is when the book with the seven seals will be revealed to them. These are the very seals which we are considering here. Their riddle will be revealed—hence the book in the centre with below it the four phases of humanity. For the four horses depict nothing other than the stages of human evolution throughout the ages.

But there is an even loftier evolution. The human being stems from yet higher worlds and he will in time reascend to those higher worlds. The form he has today will then have disappeared into the universe. What exists in the outer world today—the various 'letters' which combine to 'spell' the human being—will be absorbed by him once more. His form will have become identical with the form of the universe. In a rather trifling theosophical description there is talk of seeking God within oneself. But those who want to find God must seek him in his works spread out across the universe. Nothing in the world consists solely of matter—that is only an illusion.

In reality, all matter is an expression of spirit, an annuncia-
tion of God's activity. And the human being will, as it were,
expand over the course of times to come. He will identify
himself more and more with the universe so that one might
depict him by replacing the human form with the cosmos.

This is what we see in the fourth seal with the rocks, the
ocean and the pillars. That which today pervades the world in
the form of clouds will offer up its matter for the formation of
the human body. The forces which today are within the
spirits of the sun will in future bestow upon the human being
what will inform his spiritual forces to an infinitely loftier

degree. It is this power of the sun which the human being is striving to reach. In contrast to the plant, which directs its head, namely its roots, towards the centre of the earth, the human being directs his head towards the sun. And he will unite it with the sun and thereby receive loftier powers. This you can see depicted in the sun-face resting upon the cloud-body, the rocks and the pillars. The human being will then have become his own creator; and he is surrounded by the symbol of perfected creation—the rainbow in all its colours. A similar seal is also to be found in the Apocalypse of John. It shows a book amid the clouds, and the Apocalypse states that the initiate must swallow that book. This points to a time when the human being will receive wisdom not only from outside himself but by permeating himself with it as he permeates himself with nourishment today; and he will then have become an embodiment of wisdom.

The time then approaches when great changes are taking place in the cosmos. When the human being has drawn the power of the sun towards himself, the stage of evolution begins in which the sun is once more united with the earth. The human being will be a being of the sun. Through the power of the sun he will bring a sun to birth—hence [in the

fifth seal] the woman giving birth to the sun. So then humanity will have evolved morally and ethically to such an extent that all ruinous powers resting in the human being's lower nature will have been overcome. This is shown in the beast with seven heads and ten horns. Beneath the feet of the sun-woman is the moon which now contains all the evil substances no longer needed by the earth but not yet eliminated. All those magical forces which the moon nowadays still brings to bear on the earth will then have been overcome. When the human being has become united with the sun he will have overcome the moon.

And then [in the sixth seal] we are shown how the human being, having ascended to lofty spirituality, has come to resemble Michael and how he has shackled all the world's evil, as depicted in the symbol of the dragon.

We have, in a way, been shown that similar conditions of transformation reign both at the beginning and at the end of human evolution. We saw these conditions depicted in the man with feet of molten ore and the sword projecting from his mouth. Now, with profound symbolism, we are shown the overall existence of the world revealed in the symbol of the Holy Grail. I would like to consider this seventh seal with you in a few brief words.

Those who learn about our world from the occult point of view know that space, for the physical world, is something entirely other than an empty void. Space is the source from which all beings have, as it were, been crystallized out. Imagine an entirely transparent cube-shaped glass vessel filled with water. And now imagine that certain cooling currents are sent through the water causing multifarious shapes to form in ice. This will give you an idea of the universe being created. First there is 'space'; and then the divine creative word is uttered into this space so that all things and all beings are crystallized out.

This space, into which the divine creative word is uttered, is depicted by the occultist as a transparent cube of water. Various beings come into existence within this space. Those which are closest to us can most easily be characterized as follows.

The cube has three directions which are vertical to one another: length, height, breadth. So the cube depicts the three dimensions of space. And now imagine that these three

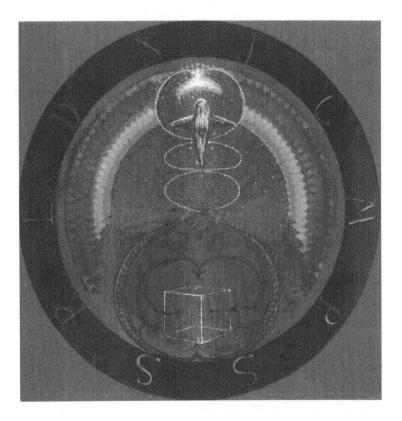

dimensions of physical space also have counter-dimensions. One way of picturing this is to think of a person walking in one direction and another walking towards him in the opposite direction. They collide. In a similar way, each spatial dimension has a counter-dimension, which gives us a total of six rays. These counter-rays represent the primordial germs of the human being's loftiest members. The physical body, crystallized out of space, is the lowest. That which is spiritual, the loftiest, is its counterpart; it is depicted as the counter-dimension.

In evolution, these counter-dimensions initially form a

being which can best be described by combining them into the world of passions, urges, instincts. This is initially what this world is. Later it becomes something different. It becomes ever more purified—we have seen the heights it reaches. But its point of departure lies in the lower urges symbolized by the snake. This process is symbolized by the meeting of the counter-dimensions in the form of two snakes coming up against one another.

As humanity becomes more purified it ascends to what we call 'the world spiral'. The purified body of the snake, this world spiral, is profoundly significant. The following example will give you an idea of what is meant. Modern astronomy is based on two theorems of Copernicus; but it ignores the third one. That one states that the sun also moves. The sun moves in a helix, so that the earth moves with the sun in a complicated curve. The same applies to the moon which moves round the earth. These movements are far more complicated than is assumed in elementary astronomy.

You can see here what significance the spiral has for the bodies of the universe; and these bodies represent a figure with which the human being will eventually be identified. When that time comes the human being will have purified his productive powers; the larynx will then be the organ of reproduction. That which the human being will have developed as the purified body of the snake will then no longer work from below upwards but from above downwards. The transformed larynx in us will become the chalice which we call the Holy Grail. And just as the one is purified, so will the other be purified, that other which is combined with this reproductive organ. It will be an essence of the universal power, the great universal essence. And this universal spirit is depicted in its essence in the image of the dove confronting the Holy Grail face to face. This is the symbol of that spiritualized impregnation which will work from out of the cosmos when the human being has become identified with the cosmos. The creative element of this process is depicted in the rainbow: this is the all-embracing seal of the Holy Grail.

This as a whole presents the significance of the connection between world and man in a wonderful way which summarizes the meaning of the other seals. That is also why the words of the world mystery are written around the outer circle of this seal. This world mystery shows how in the beginning the human being was born out of the primeval forces of the world. Every individual has at the beginning of time gone through that process which he will go through spiritually when he is reborn out of the forces of consciousness. Rosicrucianism expresses this with the letters E.D.N.: Out of God am I born.[*]

As we have seen, there is also a second element in what is revealed: in life there is death. But in order to rediscover life within this death, the human being must, in the primal source of all life, overcome this death of the senses. And that primal source lies at the centre of all cosmic evolution; for we were obliged to seek death in order to gain our consciousness. And we shall overcome it when, in the mystery of the Redeemer, we discover the meaning of this death. Just as we

---

[*] 'Ex Deo nascimur'. The following abbreviations stand for: 'In Christo morimur' and 'Per Spiritum Sanctum reviviscimus'.

are born out of God, so, as esoteric wisdom tells us, do we die in Christ: I.C.M.

And wherever something is revealed a duality becomes manifest which must be united with a third element, so the human being, once he has overcome death, will identify himself with the spirit (the dove) which permeates the world. He will rise again and will live in the spirit: P.S.S.R.

This is the theosophical Rose Cross. It shines forth into the time when religion and science will have become reconciled.

So you see how the whole world is made manifest in such seals, and because magicians and initiates have placed the world into them they possess a mighty power. You can return again and again to these seals; and you will always find that through meditation they will disclose immeasurable wisdom. Their influence on the human soul is so powerful because they have been called up from out of world mysteries. If you display them in a room where such things are being discussed in the way we are discussing them today, when one is striving towards the holy mysteries of the world, they will have a remarkably enlivening, illuminating effect, even if those present do not necessarily realize this.

On the other hand, because they have such a high degree of significance, it is not suitable to treat them with irreverence. It may seem strange, but if they are displayed in a room where no discussion of spiritual matters is going on, where trivialities are spoken, they also have an influence, but that influence harms the physical organism. This may sound trite, but their effect is to damage the digestive system. Things that have been born out of the spirit belong to the spirit; they should not be treated disrespectfully. This shows in the effect they have. Emblems of spiritual things should be placed where spiritual things are taking place and exercising their influence.

2. The Rosicrucian Schooling Path and the Rose Cross Meditation—Developing the Images

On many occasions the external world has discovered indications of Rosicrucianism in two works which stem from the early part of the seventeenth century.[8] The so-called *Fama Fraternitatis* was published in 1614, and one year later the so-called *Confessio* also appeared—two books about which there have been many disputes in scholarly circles. As with many writings, these disputes were not only concerned with whether Valentin Andreae, who in later life was a perfectly ordinary dean, could in fact have written such a book. The other argument was about whether the books had been taken seriously by their authors or whether they had merely been poking fun at the possibility of there being such a thing as a secretive brotherhood of the Rose Cross that followed certain tendencies and goals.

In the wake of these writings there are, in addition, a good number which tell all manner of things pertaining to Rosicrucianism. When you have a look at Valentin Andreae's writings, but also at other works connected with Rosicrucianism, you will, if you are unfamiliar with the movement's foundations, not find anything relevant in them. Right up to our time it has indeed not been possible to discover even the most elementary information with regard to this spiritual movement which has existed since the fourteenth century and still exists today. Whatever has been written and printed about it consists of disconnected fragments, items which have gone astray and been made public through betrayal and which are inaccurate and often distorted as a result of charlatanism, deception, ignorance or stupidity.

In true, genuine Rosicrucianism there have, since its inception, been only communications passed on verbally to those who have been sworn to secrecy. Therefore nothing of consequence has ever entered into publicly accessible literature. There are certain elementary facts concerning Rosicrucianism which can today be publicly communicated and with which we shall be concerned here. But only when one knows these things can one make any sense of those other, frequently grotesque, often merely laughable but also often fraudulent and rarely accurate disclosures in the literature.

Rosicrucianism is one of the methods whereby one can achieve initiation. We have here already often discussed what is meant by initiation. Initiation involves awakening those faculties that lie dormant in every human soul, faculties that enable one to look into the spiritual worlds which exist behind the world of the senses and of which our sense world is solely an external expression, an effect. An initiate is an individual who has worked his way through the precisely determined and scientifically developed methods of initiation, methods which have been just as scientifically worked out as are those of chemistry, physics or any other scientific field. What is worked through in such methods cannot, however, be applied to something external; it is applied solely to one's self, to the instrument, the tool by means of which one can look into the spiritual world. Those who really know

the spirit are aware of how profound and true are these words
by Goethe:

> We snatch in vain at Nature's veil,
> She is mysterious in broad daylight,
> No screws or levers can compel her to reveal
> The secrets she has hidden from our sight.[9]

How profound indeed are the secrets of nature, yet they
are not as unfathomably deep as those would claim who are
too easygoing to penetrate further into them. They are not
unfathomably profound, for they can be fathomed by the
human spirit—only not by one's everyday spirit but by that
spirit which, with the help of strictly defined methods, calls
forth from itself the hidden powers of the soul. When an
individual gradually prepares himself he will eventually reach
the point at which is revealed to him that knowledge which is
only granted to those who are genuinely initiated: that
immense secret which, to use Goethe's expression, 'binds the
world in its innermost life'.[10] Actually, the fruit of genuine
initiation is the unveiling of this secret.

As has often been explained here, the initial stages of
initiation do not pose any threat to the pupil. But the higher
stages call for the utmost devotion and the most uncondi-
tional search for the truth. When one approaches the portals
through which one can glimpse entirely other worlds, one
realizes that there is some truth in the frequently repeated
statement that it is dangerous to reveal the holiest mysteries
of existence to large numbers of people. The degree to which
it has been possible to prepare human beings gradually to
find their way to the highest secrets of nature and the spiritual

world, that is the degree to which these secrets can be revealed today.

The spiritual-scientific movement, as it is called, is one path which can lead people towards higher secrets. There are a number of such paths. But it is not the case that the ultimate wisdom to which human beings can aspire exists in a variety of forms. There is only one form of the ultimate wisdom. Wherever and whenever human beings live or have lived, once they have attained the highest wisdom, then this ultimate wisdom is identical for all human beings, just as the view from a mountain top, once one has reached the summit, is identical for all. But there is a variety of paths which can lead to the summit and the one to chose is the one that is best suited to one's own point of departure. Having reached a certain point on one's way up the mountain, if there is a suitable path to be taken just there, then it is not necessary to walk all the way round the mountain first. The same applies to the path which leads to ultimate knowledge. One's point of departure is chosen in accordance with one's own nature.

Too little attention is paid to this nowadays. The great variety in human nature must be taken into account. The higher spiritual members in the make-up of ancient Indians, although perhaps not as regards less subtle anatomy or physiology, were organized differently in comparison with today, so that for those higher members of ancient Indian individuals it was possible, even until today, to preserve a wonderful wisdom, secret or spiritual, including its relevant method of initiation: what we term the yoga-schooling. This oriental yoga-schooling is the path that leads to the summit of wisdom in the natural make-up of members of the ancient

Indian peoples. For Europeans of today the same path would be a nonsense resembling, indeed, someone arriving at the foot of a mountain and then walking all the way round it in order to find and then use a path. The natural make-up of present-day Europeans is entirely different from that of people in the ancient Orient. And similarly the human being's natural make-up during the time when Christianity was coming into being, a few centuries prior to it, and a few thereafter, was quite different from what it is today.

If we take into account what has just been said, namely that initiation involves accessing inner powers, awakening inner powers by specific methods, thus enabling the human being himself to become the instrument through which he can look into the spiritual world and make discoveries there, then we shall have to admit that account must be taken of the inner nature of the human being. The holy Rishis of old, those former great teachers of the ancient Indian peoples, developed that wonderful method which still possesses some relevance for Indian peoples today. And in the early days of Christianity the Gnostic method was able to lead the seeker into spiritual realms. Similarly, for modern humanity, for an individual living in our present environment, if he fully belongs to the world of today, deriving the conditions of his existence from it, a different method will be suitable.

Thus, again and again over the course of many millennia, the great masters of wisdom who guide human destinies have revised the methods by means of which the pinnacles of wisdom can be attained. So for today's humanity, for those who have grown up in our modern conditions of existence, it has been the Rosicrucian movement which has founded the necessary methods for today. Just as was the case with former methods, it is these Rosicrucian methods which take account specifically of the current needs of modern humanity today.

It is not that the Rosicrucian methods are unchristian or indeed anti-Christian. Far from it. The schooling which Christianity brings to human beings is also provided through the Rosicrucian method. But someone pursuing a Rosicrucian schooling will also be gaining the ability to see the totality of mystery or spiritual-scientific achievements in full concord with modern culture as a whole, with modern feeling and thinking concerning the nature of spirituality. Rosicrucian methods will still be the fitting methods of initiation into spiritual life for many centuries yet to come.

On embarking upon a Rosicrucian schooling with the aim of entering into the spiritual world, the pupil will find that the following seven steps must be undertaken.[11] It is not necessary to work on them in the sequence I shall present here. Depending on the individuality of the pupil and his current needs, the teacher will select, from one or other of the steps, whatever is suitable for him, and thus build up a course of studies for his inner schooling. First let us list the seven steps of this Rosicrucian path:

1. What we call 'studying' in the Rosicrucian sense.
2. What we call acquiring imaginative thinking.
3. What we call acquiring the occult script.
4. What we describe by the unpretentious term 'making life rhythmical' or, in the true sense, 'preparing the Philosopher's Stone'. This does indeed exist, but it is not the absurd thing about which one reads in books.

5. What we call knowledge of the microcosm or knowledge of the human being's own nature.
6. What we call merging with the macrocosm or with the great external world.
7. What we call attaining divinely blessed resting in all beings.

The sequence in which these steps are accomplished depends entirely upon the individuality of the pupil. But accomplished they must be in the elementary stage of Rosicrucianism. Please regard as a kind of ideal what I have already told you about the Rosicrucian schooling as well as what I shall now describe. Do not imagine that these things can be accomplished overnight. But one must become familiar, at least in words, with the more profound content of something which initially appears to be incomprehensible. One can make a start at any moment so long as one realizes that one must have patience, energy and perseverance.

The first point, studying, may sound rather pedantic to some, but acquiring erudition is not what is meant. One does not need to be a scholar in order to become an initiate. Erudition has little to do with spiritual knowledge. Something different is meant by the studying with which we are concerned here. But nonetheless it is essential; and a truly knowledgeable Rosicrucian teacher would never introduce a pupil to the higher stages who was disinclined to work his way through the stage of studying. The stage of studying is intended to enable the pupil to develop an entirely reasonable and utterly logical way of thinking, a way of thinking which will save him, while passing through subsequent stages, from losing—as could otherwise well happen—the ground under his feet. It is essential to ensure that someone who is to enter into the spiritual world must learn about it beforehand, for it can lead one to many an erroneous path. This is a danger from which one can only escape if one has above all laid aside any tendency towards what is fantastical or illogical or in any way irrational. Those who tend toward flights of fancy involving ideas removed from reality are not suited to the spiritual world.

That is one reason. The other is that once one enters into higher worlds one is met with all kinds of perceptions that are entirely different from those surrounding us in the world of the senses. An individual who, once the inner senses of his soul have been opened up, can look into the spiritual worlds closest to our own—the worlds we speak of as the astral and spiritual worlds, the worlds out of which we are born just as we are born out of the physical world—such an individual encounters things that are profoundly different from what we perceive here in our the sense-perceptible world. Someone who is familiar with the astral or spiritual world knows how utterly different these worlds are from those he is accustomed to seeing with his eyes and hearing with his ears.

But there is one thing which is the same in all three worlds, the physical, the astral and the spiritual (Devachanic) world, and that is logical thinking. It is because logical thinking is the same in all three worlds that we can learn to apply it while we are still here in the physical world; then it can give us firm support in those other worlds. If, on the other hand, we learn to think in a way which flits about like a will-o'-the-wisp, which means that we are unable to distinguish between

fantasy and reality, treating fantasies as realities in the physical world, then we are not capable of ascending to the
higher worlds (as is, for example, the case with our physicists
who, although they have never seen atoms in our physical
world, nonetheless treat them as a reality). Just imagine what
rubbish an individual who is not accustomed to strict and
unrelenting logic would be inclined to pronounce about the
higher worlds.

We are, however, not talking about thinking in the
ordinary sense. Ordinary thinking merely involves combining sense-perceptible realities. The thinking we are referring
to has become independent of sense perceptions. Scholars
and philosophers nowadays deny the existence of any such
thinking. You can read in the works of many present-day
philosophers that human beings are not capable of thinking
in pure thoughts since they are obliged to think in thoughts
which retain at least a remnant of sense-perceptible images.
When a philosopher says such a thing it merely proves that he
himself is incapable of thinking in pure thoughts. And it
shows an indescribable lack of modesty to declare as a general incapacity something of which one is oneself not capable.

The human being has to be capable of forming thoughts
which are no longer dependent on what his eyes or ears
perceive if he wants to live in a world of pure thought, in that
world which he finds within himself when he turns his
attention away from the external world of the senses. In
spiritual science and also in Rosicrucianism this form of
thinking is termed self-generative thinking. Someone wishing
to partake in studying of this kind may turn to the books of
present-day spiritual science. What he finds there will be

combinations not of a sense-perceptible kind but thoughts stemming from higher worlds, unified thoughts which can be comprehended by anyone who does not find it necessary to remain within the customary type of present-day banal thinking.

For the first stage of Rosicrucian schooling to be made possible it is important that something which for centuries has been cultivated in close-knit circles should now be made accessible to humanity at large by means of literature and lectures. What is thus made public is nothing other than the basic tenure, the initial stage of great and immeasurable universal knowledge. As time goes on, ever more of this will flow into humanity to whom, for some decades now, this elementary part has been revealed. For you, this can provide the basis of your schooling. My books *Truth and Science* and *The Philosophy of Freedom* are intended for those of you who want to be more thorough, who want to enter into a more rigorous schooling of thinking.

These books have not been written as other books are written in which a sentence in a particular passage can be moved without more ado to another passage. These books are not accumulations of thoughts but organisms of thoughts. One thought grows like an organism, it grows organically out of the previous one. These books do not simply add one thought to the next; they resemble an organism in which a subsequent thought grows up out of a previous one.

Thoughts must grow up out of the reader, he must sense how he is propelled towards the thinking. And then he adopts this individual type of thinking, self-generative thinking, without which one cannot reach the higher stages of Rosicrucian schooling. However, this more thorough method is not absolutely necessary, for one can also quite fruitfully remain with the elementary spiritual-scientific literature that is also capable of providing the material for study.

The second stage is that of imaginative thinking. One should not embark on what I have termed imaginative thinking until one has absorbed the strict necessity of thought just described, from which one will have gained a rigorous core of knowledge. Without this it will be easy to lose the firm ground under one's feet.

So what is imaginative thinking? In his Rosicrucian epos *The Mysteries*, Goethe demonstrated how profoundly imbued he was with the secrets of Rosicrucianism. He gives an indication of this in the beautiful words from the Chorus Mysticus at the end of *Faust Part II*: 'All things transient are but a parable.'[12] This was systematically enlarged upon wherever there was an inner Rosicrucian schooling. Wherever he was in the world, a Rosicrucian had to learn to develop, as a corollary to logical thinking, a corresponding imaginative way of thinking, that way of thinking which sees the spiritual, the everlasting aspect in all that is around us.

When you meet someone who is smiling happily, you will not be satisfied with merely describing those odd contortions of his face, of his physiognomy visible to your eyes. It will be quite clear to your soul that the singular expression denoting gaiety is a revelation of the person's inner life. Similarly, if you see trickling tears you will not embark upon an inspection of what is going on because you will know that those tears are an expression of inner pain or suffering. A person's physiognomy allows you to look right into the very foundation of his soul. The Rosicrucian pupil must learn to approach the whole of nature in this way. Just as a facial expression or a gesture of the hands give expression to a human being's life of soul, so is it also with everything in nature. Just as the gesture of a person's hand means something to our soul, so, for a Rosicrucian, is everything in the world around him—rocks, plants, animals, stars, every breath of air—an expression of profound reality and not merely a picture of poetic beauty.

Everything around us thus becomes an expression of soul and spirit, not in a poetic sense but in stark reality, just as shining eyes, a puckered brow, trickling tears are expressions of inner states of soul. You will know what is meant by imaginative thinking when you understand that what Goethe says through the Earth Spirit in *Faust* is not merely a poetic image but actual reality; when you go beyond today's materialistic outlook and see a reality in what the Earth Spirit says, whereas nowadays people merely enjoy the poetic imagery:

> In life like a flood, in deeds like a storm
> I surge to and fro,
> Up and down I flow!
> Birth and the grave
> An eternal wave,
> Turning, returning,
> A life ever burning:
> At Time's whirring loom I work and play
> God's living garment I weave and display.[13]

When the words of the Earth Spirit have become a reality for you and you are not upset if materialists regard you as a fool, then you will realize that your logic is more profound than that of those materialists, for they merely think they know whereas you really do know because you stand freely before a spiritual reality. Just as truly as a human soul is revealed in facial expressions, just as an Earth Spirit lives in the physiognomy of the earth—when you see the earth's enjoyment in a plant, when the earth tells you the sorrow of the Earth Spirit as though nature were speaking to you and telling you its secrets—then, when you experience all this you will begin to spell out the earth's secrets and will understand what it means to attain imaginative thinking. Then you will reach an understanding of how, in Rosicrucianism and also in the great occult tradition of the Holy Grail, all this was presented as the purest and most beautiful expression of how imaginative thinking can be attained.

Let us cast a glance towards the true nature of this ideal of the Holy Grail. It will be shown to you in every Rosicrucian school just as I shall describe it to you now. I shall use the form of a dialogue, although such a dialogue has never actually taken place in proper Rosicrucian schools.[*] There, lengthy methods of development in life led to what I shall now summarize in the form of a dialogue which will reveal what the ideal of the Holy Grail genuinely encompasses.

Look at how the plant grows up out of the earth. It is directed towards the centre of the earth, its stem rises

[*] See also the lecture in Düsseldorf on 15 December 1907 in GA 98, pp. 50–3; lecture in Berlin on 15 October 1908 in GA 57, pp. 20f; public lecture in Berlin on 11 November 1909 in GA 58, pp. 185–91.

upwards, at the top is the flower wherein lie the fertilizing organs which will produce the seeds enabling the plant to live on beyond itself. Darwin, the great naturalist, was not the first to point out that when comparing a plant with a human being it is the root which must be compared with the head. The root of the plant equates with the head of the human being—Rosicrucian occultism said this long ago—and that which the plant chastely directs towards the sun as its calyx equates with what the human being directs downwards as his organ of fertilization. The human being is a plant in reverse. The organs which the plant chastely directs upwards towards the light are directed ashamedly downward and hidden away by the human being. The human being is a plant in reverse. This is a tenet of Rosicrucian occultism and indeed of all occultisms throughout the ages. The plant directs its organs of fertilization chastely towards the sun. The human being directs his organs of fertilization towards the centre of the earth while his head is directed in freedom towards the realm of the sun. In the middle between the two stands the animal.

These three directions, which are represented by the plant, the animal and the human being, are known as the cross. The plant is the beam which points downwards, the animal is the cross-beam, and the human being is the beam which points upwards. When Plato, that great initiate-philosopher of antiquity, states that the world-soul is crucified upon the cross of the world-body, this signifies nothing other than that the human being represents the highest configuration of the world-soul and that the world-soul has passed through the three kingdoms: the plant kingdom, the animal kingdom and the human kingdom. The world-soul is crucified upon the cross: plant kingdom, animal kingdom, human kingdom, the three kingdoms of nature—a wonderfully profound image given by Plato, spoken entirely out of spiritual science.

This image was repeated untold times in the Rosicrucian schools: 'See the plant with its head pointing downwards and its organs of fertilization held high towards the shaft of sunlight.' This shaft of sunlight was termed the holy lance of love which has permeated the plant so that the seeds shall grow and reach maturity. And then the pupil was told: 'Raise your eyes up to the human being, look at the plant and then at the human being. Compare his physical matter and substance with those of the plant. The human being is the plant in reverse and he has become like this because he has permeated his matter, his flesh with physical urges, with passion and sensuality. Chastely and in purity the plant is permitted to raise its organs of fertilization up towards the lance of fertilization, the sacred lance of love.'

The human being will have attained an equivalent position at the moment when he has entirely purified his urges. He is looking towards a future in which the ideal will be fulfilled: 'You are now as chaste and pure as the calyx of the plant. Then will you have arrived at the summit of your earthly evolution; then will impure urges no longer permeate your lower organs; then will you direct the spiritual lance of love, your power of reproduction, spiritually towards the chalice, just as the plant's calyx opens itself to the sacred lance of love in the shaft of the sun's light.'

Thus will the human being progress through the kingdoms of nature, purifying himself until those organs which are now at the outset of their evolution will have attained their ultimate development. When a human being brings forth something in what is sacred and noble, then will he be at the beginning of a future productive power which he will possess when his lower nature has been fully purified. Then will he have a new organ. The calyx of the plant will arise anew at a higher stage and be held out towards the lance of Amfortas, just as the flower's calyx is held up towards the sun's spiritual lance of love.

Thus should you imagine, on this lower level, that which, as a high ideal, will in future be given to the human race: when all that is base will have been purified and when what is chaste and untainted will have been held up to the spiritual sun of the future; when this plant-calyx will have passed through the nature of the human being, which will in a certain sense stand at a higher and in a certain sense at a lower level than the plant; when the plant-calyx will have become purified up to the highest spirituality and is held up before the spiritualized sun as the holy chalice, that elevated plant-calyx which will have passed through the stage of humanity.

This is what the Rosicrucian pupil comprehended; it is the mystery of the Holy Grail, the highest ideal it is possible to present to the human being. In this way the whole of nature comes forward glowing and flooded through with spiritual meaning. If one becomes able to comprehend everything in this way, when one sees in everything a parable of the spirit, then one is on the way to acquiring imaginative thinking. Then the colours emerge from the things and become autonomous, and the tones emerge from them and become autonomous; space becomes filled with an autonomous world of colour and sound in which the spiritual beings make known their presence. We ascend from imaginative thinking to actual knowledge of spiritual space. This is the path followed by the Rosicrucian at the second stage of his schooling.

3. The third *stage* is knowledge about the occult script. This is no ordinary script but rather one which is linked with the secrets of nature. I shall straight away clarify for you what you should regard as the occult script. One commonly known emblem of this script is the so-called whorl, the vortex. You can imagine it as two intertwined sixes. This emblem is used in order to indicate and characterize the inner nature of certain phenomena which are present in the whole of the natural and spiritual world.

When you examine a plant you will observe that it develops right up to the formation of the seed. If you then place this seed in the earth a similar plant will grow from it, identical with the previous one. To imagine that any substance from the previous plant enters into the new one is a materialistic concept which will be refuted in the future. What enters into the new plant is solely the formative power of the previous one. As far as its physical substance is concerned the old plant dies completely while the new one is something entirely new. Not even the smallest particle of physical substance is passed from the old plant to the new one. This new approach to the coming into being and dying away of a plant is indicated by drawing two intertwined spirals, in other words a vortex, without allowing the two lines to come into contact with one another.

Now, vortices of this kind are to be found both in external and in spiritual nature. For example, spiritual research shows us that a vortex or whorl of this kind was present in human

evolution when the ancient Atlantean culture was making the transition to the new, post-Atlantean culture. Spiritual science here shows you something of which only an initial, most elementary stage is known to modern science. It shows you that what is today the ocean between Europe and America was once filled with a continent, that a most ancient culture came into being there, and that the continent was then inundated by what we know as 'the Flood', and disappeared. This shows us that what Plato tells us of the submergence of the island of Poseidonis is founded on truth and that it was a remnant of the ancient Atlantean continent. That culture disappeared with regard to its spiritual characteristic, and a new culture arose; so that this process can be depicted by means of those two intertwined spirals, the vortex. What is ancient is shown as the inward-coiling spiral and what is new as the unfurling one.

When the transition from the Atlantean to the post-Atlantean culture was taking place, the sun in springtime was rising in the constellation of Cancer. You know that the sun moves forward during the course of the year. Well, in those ancient times it was rising at the beginning of spring in the constellation of Cancer. Then for a while it rose in the constellation of Gemini, then in the constellation of Taurus, and then that of Aries. Peoples have always sensed something especially beneficial in the first rays of the sun reaching them from the dome of heaven. That is how it came about that when the sun began to rise in the constellation of Aries people started to venerate the Ram—hence all the sayings about the lamb, the legend of the Golden Fleece and so on. Before the sun began to rise in the constellation of Aries it rose in the constellation of Taurus. So the cultures preceding those of the Ram venerated the Bull as the sacred animal. You will thus find, for example, that in those times the Egyptian Apis bull was venerated. In the period of transition from the Atlantean to the post-Atlantean culture you had the dominion of the constellation of Cancer. And so you find in the calendar those two intertwined whorls as the sign of the Crab.

There are hundreds, indeed thousands of these signs which one gradually learns. They are not arbitrary signs. When one has become familiar with them they show one ways of entering into things and beginning to live inside them. Just as studying takes hold of one's understanding, of one's imaginative thinking, so does knowledge of the occult script take hold of the will. It shows us the paths of creating and producing. Whereas studying and finding knowledge takes us to Imagination, so does knowledge of the occult script bring us to the magic of knowing about the things that slumber in the laws of nature, knowledge which leads us more deeply into things.

In many works—thus also in those of Eliphas Lévi—you will find many occult signs. But those who know nothing of such things will learn little from them. You do, though, gain an impression of how they come about. However, printed works about such things on the whole contain only irrelevancies. All peoples, or at least all initiates, held the signs of the occult script to be sacred. And looking further into the past we find stern rules about how they are to be kept secret, so that those who are permitted to use them never do so in an unworthy fashion. Rigorous punishments are set to deal with any infringement of those rules.

4. The fourth stage is what is known as preparing the Philosopher's Stone. What you might find about it in the pertinent literature is rather irrelevant or, usually, mostly foolish drivel. If the Philosopher's Stone were really as it is described there, we would all have the right to mock it. You will see what I mean as you follow what I am about to describe; this will give you considerable insight into the matter.

Towards the end of the eighteenth century a serious journal in central Germany published an article about the Philosopher's Stone. When reading this article, those who know something about these matters gain the impression that the writer had indeed at some point heard something about it. His words are perfectly correct, but one realizes that he himself fails to understand them properly. He writes: 'The Philosopher's Stone is something with which all human beings are familiar, something which most individuals have held in their hands many, many times, something which can be found in many places on the earth, but which people do not realize is the Philosopher's Stone.' This is, indeed, a peculiar description of the Philosopher's Stone, and yet word for word it is true. One must try to reach a proper understanding of what is meant.

Consider the process of human breathing; what is described as finding or creating the Philosopher's Stone is linked with a regulation of the breathing process. Nowadays the human being inhales oxygen and exhales carbon dioxide; a combination of oxygen and carbon dioxide is exhaled. The human being inhales oxygen, the air of life, and exhales carbon dioxide, an actual poison. Neither the human being nor the animal can live with this carbon dioxide. If the animals, which breathe in the same way as human beings, were to exist alone on the earth, and if they had always breathed as they do today, they would have thoroughly poisoned the air around them so that neither animals nor man would nowadays be able to breathe.

How is it, then, that they can indeed still breathe? It is because the plant absorbs the carbon dioxide, retaining the carbon within it and releasing the oxygen so that humans and animals alike can once again use the oxygen for breathing. The result is a decent process of interchange between the breathing of the animal and human world and the breathing—or assimilation process—of the plant world. I use the term assimilation so that pedantic scholars have no reason to object. Someone earning five marks every day and spending only two can talk of making a profit; his situation differs from that of someone spending five marks daily while earning two. The situation as regards breathing can be similar. But the important point is that the process of exchange between the human being and the world of plants exists.

This process of exchange is very remarkable. So let us take another, closer look. Oxygen enters into the human body and out of the human body comes carbon dioxide. The plant retains the carbon and returns the oxygen to the human being. In the coal dug up out of the ground billions of years after the coming into being of the plant in question you can once again see the carbon breathed in by that plant. The everyday process of breathing which takes place as described shows how necessary the plant is today for the life of the human being and how in that process of breathing something takes place within him which is only half a process. He needs the plant as something which is not inside him so that it can transform the carbon into oxygen for him.

There thus exists a making-rhythmical of the breathing process in the Rosicrucian sense, but communication about this in more detail can only take place from one person to another. It can be hinted at here only in a manner which refrains from going into any detail. The Rosicrucian pupil received, and still receives, certain instructions about breathing in a specific way, in a specific rhythm and with specific thought forms. Thus his breathing process is transmuted.

You can only imagine this transmutation by taking note of the saying: A constant drip will hollow the stone. Even in the case of the most elevated personage the internal life processes cannot be transformed from one day to the next through breathing in the Rosicrucian manner. Breathing in this way brings about a specific change in the body of the human being. This change means that in future this individual becomes capable of transforming the carbon dioxide into usable oxygen within himself. What today takes place outside him in the plant, the transformation of carbon into oxygen (which today the plant does on behalf of the human being), will in the future—when the breathing process continues on in this way in the one who is to become an initiate—be brought about by an organ of his own, an organ as yet unknown to physiology and anatomy but which is never-theless already in the process of being developed. So the human being will then bring about this transmutation him-self. Instead of exhaling the carbon and giving it to the plant he will use it within himself, building up his own body with the help of the carbon which he previously had to pass on to the plant.

Consider now what I have just described and combine it with what I have said about the ideal of the Holy Grail, namely that the pure, chaste plant nature will have passed through the nature of the human being, and that this nature of the human being will, in its highest spirituality, have arrived once again in the plant of today. The day will come when the human being will be capable of bringing about the plant process within himself. Out of the substances at present within him he will increasingly create that ideal in which his body becomes a plant body which will be the bearer of a far higher and more spiritual consciousness. In this way the pupil learns to bring about the alchemy which makes him capable of transforming the fluids and substances of the human being into carbon. What today is done by the plant which builds up its body out of carbon will in future be achieved by the human being himself. He will create a bodily structure out of carbon, and this will be the future structure of the human body.

There is a great mystery hidden behind what we term the making-rhythmical of the breathing process. So you will now understand the hint about the Philosopher's Stone contained in the note I quoted just now.

What does the human being learn with regard to the

building up of his future bodily form? He learns how to create ordinary carbon, which is also the stuff of diamonds, in order to build up his body with it. In a raised and enhanced consciousness he will become able to garner this carbon out of himself and use it within himself. He will become capable of forming his own substance which is built upon the plant substance founded on the structure of carbon. This is the alchemy which will lead to the creation of the Philosopher's Stone. The human body is itself the retort transformed in the sense suggested just now.

Thus, behind the regulation of the breathing process, which is often described in connection with the Philosopher's Stone in an entirely nonsensical way, there does indeed lie what is called the discovery or the preparation of the Philosopher's Stone. These are the hints from the Rosicrucian schools which have only recently been made public. In books you will search for them in vain. This is a small part of the fourth stage: the search for the Philosopher's Stone.

The fifth stage consists in what is termed knowledge of the microcosm, of the small world. This leads us back to what Paracelsus said, something to which I have frequently made reference. All things which surround us would, if we could make an extract of them, present us with the human being. The human being has within himself those substances and forces which manifest as a brief recapitulation of the whole of nature. So when we see nature all around us we can say that what is out there represents the great archetype of what is within us as a copy.

Let us take light as an example. What has this light brought about in the human being? If the human eye did not exist we would be unaware of light. The world would be for us gloomy and dark. When animals make their lives in dark caves, for example the Caves of Kentucky, they lose the power of sight. The eye itself is created by light. We would have no eyes if light did not exist. It is light which enticed our organs of sight to emerge from our skin, from our organism. Goethe said that the eye is made by light and for light; and the ear is made by sound and for sound.

All things are born out of the great world, out of the macrocosm. Upon this rests the mystery of how, through certain instructions, certain directives, by going more deeply into our body, we become able to fathom not only the spiritual world but also the nature which surrounds us. If under certain conditions and with certain forms of thought we enter meditatively into the inmost aspects of the eye, we learn to recognize the inmost essential nature of light.

Between the eyebrows and the bridge of the nose there lies a point which is highly relevant in this connection. By immersing oneself in it, one learns about significant and important processes in the spiritual world which were taking place when this part of the head was coming into being out of the surrounding world. In this way one learns about how the human being was pieced together spiritually. The human being has been formed entirely out of spiritual beings and spiritual forces. So by immersing himself in his own form he learns to recognize the spiritual beings and the spiritual forces that have built and formed his organism.

There is something else which must also be said in this connection. This immersion of oneself into the innermost part of the human being, and also those exercises which work their way downwards into the bodily nature, which involve working into the physical body from the I—the atman*— should not be undertaken without prior preparation. When one begins to work with these things it is necessary to have done prior spiritual work. That is why the Rosicrucian schooling involves a strict schooling of thoughts. The pupil must also have a strong morality for this schooling, a firm inner core. If he lacks these he is liable to founder. He can immerse himself meditatively in every member of his being, and worlds will open up within him. No one can become acquainted with the true nature of the Old Testament without thus immersing himself in the true inner nature of his being; but this must be done in accordance with specific rules which can be given to him through spiritual-scientific schooling.

All these things are written about from out of spiritual science, from out of insights into the spiritual world. That is why they can only become comprehensible if one is capable of searching for them within one's own being. The human being has been born out of the macrocosm, and as a microcosm he must find within himself the forces and laws at work there. One cannot find the human being within oneself by being an anatomist. One can only find oneself by learning to look into one's own inner being which will then shine and resound in its different parts. Every organ has its own specific colour and its own specific sound once the whole has become exposed to the inward-looking soul. Having learned through

---

* Rudolf Steiner here linked the Hindu word 'atman' (soul) with the German 'Atem' (breath). Tr.

the Rosicrucian schooling what has been created within one out of the macrocosm, one can then begin to recognize the things which are in that macrocosm. When one has come to know one's inner being through immersing oneself in one's eye, or in that point above the bridge of the nose, then one can look outwards and recognize spiritually the great laws of the macrocosm. Through one's own perception one can then recognize spiritually what an inspired genius wrote in the Old Testament; one sees it in the Akashic Records and is thus enabled to follow up the evolution of humanity over millions of years.

All this can be truly understood through a schooling such as this. It is a schooling which differs from any ordinary schooling. Do not believe that self-knowledge can be attained by means of haphazard brooding within yourself, or that when you look into yourself the god in your inner being will begin to speak to you, as is so often taught nowadays. No, one must immerse oneself in one's organs in order then to recognize the great self of the world. The saying known throughout time is true: 'Know yourself.' But it is equally true that one's higher self cannot come to be known through one's own inner nature. For this, as Goethe, that great seer said, one must expand one's spirit so that it becomes a universe.

This is what takes place at the sixth stage of Rosicrucian schooling as one patiently treads one's path. It is not an easy path. One has to delve down into one's inner being. One cannot be satisfied with platitudes and generalizations. One must enter into every being, taking it lovingly into oneself. Any complacency must be abhorrent. One must immerse oneself in the beings, getting to know them quite concretely in all their specific qualities. There can be no carrying on about such things as: the harmony of the world; becoming at one with the world soul; mingling with the universe. Such catchphrases have no value in the Rosicrucian schooling which does not chatter on about being at one with infinity or suchlike. Its aim is to enliven the forces of the human soul.

When an individual has endeavoured to expand his self in this way, the seventh stage of the soul will no longer be far away. This is where knowledge is transformed into feeling, where what lives in the soul is transformed into feeling and one ceases to have that sense of being solely within oneself. One begins to feel that one is within every being. When we have become immersed in every stone, in every plant, in every animal we then feel what the plant, what the stone and what the animal feels, and every separate thing reveals itself to us in its very being, not through words, not through concepts but with innermost feeling. The time then begins when we become bound up in a general network of sympathy with all beings, where we live our way into all beings.

This living one's way into all beings is what is termed the seventh stage: divinely blessed resting in all beings. When a human being feels himself to be bound up with all other beings, when he no longer lives within his skin but has entered into all beings, when he shares what all beings feel, when he has expanded to fill the space of the whole universe in a way which allows him to say 'You are all this', when he has become all feeling, all blissfulness, then the moment has come when it is appropriate to say what Goethe, based on the Rosicrucian schooling, said in his poem *The Mysteries*:

Who combined roses with the cross?

This may be said not only from the highest standpoint but also from the very first step towards taking as one's watchword that which is expressed in the rose-entwined cross. What the cross expresses is that the human being overcomes the self about which he broods and which is only his lower self, the self which can never become aware of his higher self; he escapes from the lower self and is taken up into the higher self which leads him joyously into the living and weaving of all beings once he has come to understand what is written in Goethe's *Divan of West and East*:

> And so long you have not this,
> This dying and becoming,
> You'll be but a gloomy guest
> On the dark earth turning.

Yes indeed. If we are unable to comprehend this narrowly limited self and this emergence into the higher self, if we cannot understand that symbol of dying and becoming, the withering of the lower self and the flowering of the roses of the higher self, then we shall be unable to understand Goethe's motto through which we may determine the objectivity of Rosicrucianism, the watchword, the sign of the seven members which must stand above the rose-entwined cross:

> From the power that binds all beings
> That man is free who overcomes himself.[14]

The true esoteric significance of the cross symbol is a sum of forces. One of the forces has a downward direction: the being of the plant is governed by this force.[15] For the human being the opposite direction applies. The animal with its horizontal spine shows the force circling the earth horizontally. The soul principle rises from plant existence to animal existence, and to human existence. [...]

Development towards becoming a human being occurs through the pure, chaste plant substance becoming permeated with urges, instincts and passions. The human being gains his consciousness, he becomes human, by passing through the animal nature. By weaving the lower nature of passion into the chaste plant nature he has risen from dull plant consciousness to bright, daytime consciousness.

From this stage of present-day humanity the teacher made the pupil aware of a higher stage. Just as the human being has developed upwards from the plant stage, so will he eventually also purify his instincts and urges towards a higher, chaste stage. The teacher showed the pupil the predispositions within his physical body through which the higher stages of consciousness can be attained and through which the human substance can furthermore become a substance similar to that of the plant. Every creature must have a physical body if it wants to appear on the earth. And the body of the human being will in future undergo ever more changes.

With regard to the organs of the human being we distinguish between a descending and an ascending development. One part of the human being is undergoing a descending development; this part will, as time goes on, after many millennia, be discarded by the human being. Other organs are in the process of being developed; in future they will undergo an ascending development as will, for example, the larynx which is at present in the early stage of its evolution. Another ascending development will be undergone by the human heart, which will in future become an entirely different organ. Whereas other organs have already passed their zenith and are being pinched off from human nature as they shrivel, we have in the heart an organ which is only at the outset of its evolution.

In human muscles we can distinguish between striated and smooth muscles. These are voluntary and involuntary muscles. The voluntary muscles in, for example, the hand are striated. Conversely, the muscles of the intestines which involuntarily move the food along are smooth. The heart is the exception. For physiologists and anatomists this is a puzzle. The heart is one of the involuntary muscles, and yet its muscles are striated. That is why our anatomists are unable to comprehend the heart. They regard all organs as being of the same kind, and when one considers them spiritually they may indeed consist of the same components chemically. And yet one of them may be in a descending development while the other is in an ascending development. The heart is on the way to becoming a voluntary muscle, so in its anatomical structure it already bears the relevant characteristic attributes.

Little of this is in evidence as yet. But it already contributes to the way experiences of the soul influence the blood. You can see how sensations of fear withdraw it from the periphery of the body and send it to the interior, or how when you are ashamed it is driven from the interior to the periphery. In the future, apart from this reconfiguration of the heart a reconfiguration of the larynx will also come about.

Today the larynx serves to convert my thoughts into words by bringing about vibrations in the air. You can take in my words with your ears and listen to them; this is brought about by the vibrations in the air. The human larynx of today is able to convert what takes place in the soul into vibrations of the air. The human body of the future will transform its larynx into an organ of fertilization. Then the word which at present is only creative in the air will become creative in our environment. Reproduction will then be accomplished by the larynx, which will bring into being the human race of the future.

The teacher drew the pupil's attention to the chaste calyx of the plant, and he indicated how, in his descending phase, the human being permeated his plant substance with the base nature of passions, urges and instincts, whereby he was able to exchange these for his present-day clear daytime conscious-ness. In the same way the teacher showed how the present-day human being will rise up to higher states of consciousness and how the future human being will transform the passion-filled substance into pure and chaste organs.

The pupil was shown the past, the present and the future. He was shown how the plant chastely extends its calyx towards the sun and how its organs of fructification grow up towards the sun. This will come about once again at a higher level when the human being extends his larynx like a chalice towards the spiritual rays of the sun. This spiritual chalice, this transformed organ of speech, was termed the Holy Grail. This is a true ideal. In the beginning, the middle and the end of human evolution you are shown the concept of human evolution transformed into an image.

The feelings we develop by contemplating these images engender the strength which can truly render the higher worlds accessible to us. There is no magical hocus-pocus in this. Through the pictures the feelings are stimulated which lead the human being into the higher worlds. Feelings and sensibilities lead the human being into the astral world, just as the will leads him into the Devachanic or spiritual world. Thinking corresponds with the physical world, feeling with the astral world, and the purified will with the world of Devachan. When we look at a plant in its original chaste substance we find green as the colour of plant life. In the parts where the ether body is alive the plant is filled with the green of the leaves, which we term chlorophyll. The ether body is subject to a fundamental law, the law of repetition. If the ether body alone were active in the plant, it would again and again repeat one and the same form; it would sprout one leaf after the other. When the earth's astral body begins to influence the plant it ceases to grow and develops the flower. The effect of the ether body is revealed in repetition. And this principle also influences human growth. The ether body shows its influence in the formation of the vertebrae which, however, ceases when the astral body begins to work as the capsule of the skull is formed.

Thus we can only influence the ether body by means of the principle of repetition. When you think and comprehend, this affects solely the astral body. But when, for example, you pray or meditate, repeating the same prayer or the same meditation every day, then you are also working into the ether body. The matter is such that in the cosmos the principle of repetition is the first to be discernible through the deeds of the ether body, and then the principle of termination shows through the astral body. And where the astral body withdraws it goes without saying that the principle of repetition reappears. That is why hair and nails continue to grow; for there the astral body has withdrawn. And it is not painful to cut your hair since pain is an expression of the astral body.

Initially there is the pure, chaste plant substance where the plant, obeying only the law of the ether body, grows one leaf after the other. And then this pure, chaste plant substance is permeated more and more by what in theosophy is termed *kama*, that which is bound by instinct and feeling, the realm of urges right up to concepts. And now, in the human being, what has been developing in him since the time when his nature was plantlike must be overcome. By advancing in his development the human being has absorbed the red blood into himself. The red blood brings it about that he becomes conscious of himself. It is the chlorophyll of the plant, permeated by astral substance and the I, that has been transformed into the red blood. If you were able to permeate the green plant substance with the I and the astral substance, you would have the red blood in consequence.

So now think of the image of the cross. The image of the cross also contains something which points towards the future of humanity. What is the human being's future? He must regain the plant nature, but it must be linked with the higher stage of consciousness that today's human being has already attained. The red roses of the Rose Cross indicate what he has attained through the blood, but also what he once had and must have again by way of the plant nature. This is prefigured in the rose. It possesses the plant nature but also the red colour of the blood. The ether body is at work in the green leaves; and the astral body is at work where completion is, in the red flower. The flower of the rose owes its red to the most intensive impact of the earth's astral body.

The human being's astral body will become free and will work consciously from the outside, from outside the physical body, just as today the astral body of the earth works on the rose. And then what is now the plant rose at a lower stage will appear at a higher stage as the human rose. So here, in the wreath of roses surrounding the black wood of the cross we shall indeed have an indication pointing to the evolution of the human being. In the black wood we see what is dying; it is an image of what will also die within the human being. And in the red rose we see what will continue to develop right up to that chalice which will—like the calyx of the plant pointing towards the sun—raise itself towards the spiritual rays of the sun. The Rose Cross, where the red roses surround the black cross, gives us an image of that process.

The important thing about symbols is that we do not only think them but also feel and sense them. When we feel that the red rose is saying to us, 'See what you will one day become, see what is the aim of human evolution,' and when our heart opens and our feelings become pure, then will the forces be released in us which lead us up to a higher world. This is how these symbols are at work upon our soul. They fill our soul with strength, they thoroughly work into our soul, they are the greatest and most powerful educators of our humankind.

[handwritten: Summary so far?]

The first stage of knowledge reaching beyond our ordinary thinking is called Imaginative knowing.[16] The second stage is Inspired knowing, and the third stage is what we call Intuitive knowing. How, then, does the first stage of knowing come about? What do we do in our soul in order to develop higher forces of knowing? [...] *[handwritten: How the first stage of knowing comes about.]*

We have often mentioned the example which helps us understand what Imaginative knowing is. It is an example of the methods applied to himself by the student of spiritual science. It is an example among many others that can best be depicted in the form of a dialogue between teacher and pupil. *[handwritten: Imaginative Knowing described]*

The teacher aiming to educate a pupil in those higher forms of thinking that lead to Imagination would say to his pupil: 'Look at this plant. It grows up out of the ground and unfolds leaf after leaf until it reaches the flower. Compare this plant with a human being standing before you. This human being possesses something which is more advanced than the plant; he is in a certain sense ahead of the plant in that the world is mirrored in his ideas, his feelings and sensitivities. He is more advanced than the plant in that he possesses what one can term human consciousness. However, he has been obliged to attain this human consciousness at a price; on his way to becoming human he has had to take into himself passions, urges and desires which can lead him into error, injustice and iniquity. The plant simply grows in accordance with its inborn laws; it unfolds its nature in accordance with these inborn laws, so that—short of being fantasists—we cannot attribute to it any passions, urges or desires which might distract it from its proper path.'

But if we now consider the outer expression of the human

being's life of consciousness, of his I—if we consider the blood circulating within him as does the green chlorophyll fluid in the plant, then we have to say: As the blood circulates and pulses through the human being it is just as much an expression of his elevation to higher stages of consciousness as it is of his passions and urges which drag him down.

So now the teacher of spiritual science might say to his pupil: 'Imagine to yourself how the human being is continuing to develop so that through his I he becomes able to conquer error and evil and ugliness and everything that seeks to drag him down into evil, and how he purifies and cleanses his emotions and passions. Imagine the concrete ideal for which the human being is striving, so that his blood is no longer an expression of various passions but rather of that within him which can conquer everything that drags him down. In such a case his red blood can be compared with what in the plant has developed out of the green plant fluids to become the red rose. Just as the red rose shows us the plant juices in all their purity, bringing before us at a more perfect stage what the plant was at a less perfect stage, so would the red blood in a purified and chastened human being depict for us what comes into being when he has gained dominion over everything that drags him down.'

These are the feelings and conceptions which the spiritual teacher can awaken in the soul and mind of his pupil. If the pupil in spiritual matters is no dry-as-dust or prosaic _ordinary_ old stick, if he can feel and sense the whole mystery of what is pictured in such a comparison, then it will work upon his soul; when this symbol of spiritual experience appears before his soul it will be a genuine experience for him. The Rose

7-Headed Beast has 4 animals { Lion, Bull, Human (Angel), Eagle } where the human fails to live up to his goodness, his Astral body looks like a 7-headed beast, 3 animals get added to the o four

Cross can be a symbol of this kind. The black cross is an expression of what has been slain in the lower nature of the human being; and the roses, like the red blood, are cleansed and purified until they become a chaste expression of the higher soul within him. Thus the black cross entwined with red roses becomes a symbolic summary of what the soul experiences in that conversation between the pupil and his spiritual teacher.

When the pupil of the spirit, with the blood of his soul, has won for himself such a symbol—after permitting all the concepts and feelings to work upon his soul in such a way that they justify within him an overall view of the Rose Cross—when he not only sees himself confronted by a rose-entwined cross but has within himself the essence of a higher, inner soul mood struggled for by his bleeding soul, then he will see how such an image and, indeed other, similar images, brings something to the surface in his soul. This is then no longer merely a tiny spark in his spirit but a whole new power of knowledge enabling him to see the world in a new way. He has not remained merely the individual he had become in his life hitherto; he has developed his soul to a higher level. And if he repeats this again and again he will finally reach the Imaginative knowing which shows him that there is something else out there in the world. Thus he develops a new kind of knowing over against that kind of knowing which he would have possessed had he ceased in his efforts at the previous stage.

So now let us put before our soul how this path came about. Did the human being say to himself: 'I am treading the outward path and seeking for the foundations of things?' This is only a part of what he said. What he does say is: 'I am entering into the world outside myself, but I am not searching for the foundations of things, I am not looking for molecules and atoms, and I am not even taking from the world outside me what is on offer for me there; but I do retain a hold on something which is offered to me by the world outside.' The black cross is not something that would come into being in the soul if the wood did not exist outside; and the red rose is something which the soul would never be capable of constructing if it did not have an external impression of that red rose. In this way what is present in the content of the soul has been gathered in from the outside world.

Unlike the mystic, we cannot claim to have erased everything belonging to the outside world or to have turned our attention entirely away from the outside world. What we can say is that we have taken from the outside world what it can itself give us; we have not closed our eyes to the outside world, but neither have we taken it exactly as it was offered, for nowhere in the world is there in reality such a thing as a Rose Cross. We have formed the symbol of the Rose Cross out of what is present in the outside world; but the Rose Cross itself does not exist in the outside world.

So what motivated us to combine these two, the rose and the wood, and create a symbol out of them? The motivation came from our work on our own soul. We have what we can experience in our own soul when we turn it towards the outside world, and we have what we can experience in the outside world if we do not merely stare at it from the outside but immerse ourselves in it. And then we experience mystically what arises out of comparing the plant with the developing human being. We have refrained from directly absorbing this soul experience in the way a mystic would have done. Instead, we have offered the experiences of our soul to what the outside world can contribute and, with the help of what the soul can contribute inwardly, we have created a symbol.

The symbol contains a confluence of a mystical internal life and an external life. We may never claim that the Rose Cross is a truth either with regard to the sense-perceptible world or with regard to our internal world, for no one would be capable of constructing a Rose Cross in his internal world if he lacked any impressions from the external world. The symbol contains a confluence of what the soul can experience and come to know out of its inner life with that which it can receive from outside. That is why this symbol now stands before us in such a way that it leads us neither directly into the external world nor directly into the internal world; instead, it functions like a force. When we place it before our soul in meditation it brings a new spiritual eye into being so that we can now look into the spiritual world which we have formerly been unable to find either inwardly or outwardly. So we now begin to have an intimation that what lies at the foundation of the external world and what we can now experience through Imaginative knowing is one and the same as what we also have in our own inner being.

If we now move up to Inspired knowing we must first divest ourselves of our image. We must now do something which is directly reminiscent of the whole way in which a mystic works when he goes inwards. We now have to forget

both the rose and the wood of the cross. It is a difficult thing
to do, but it can be done. We must banish from our mental
image the whole content of the symbol. Although it is difficult to do, we must succeed.

An activity of soul was needed in order to bring the above
comparison before the soul as a symbol. We must now
observe the soul itself, in what it did in order to bring the
black cross before the soul as the human being who must be
conquered and in order to bring into view its inner experiences in forming symbols. When the human being mystically
immerses himself in his soul experiences he comes to the
stage of Inspired knowing. And then he experiences in a new
capacity, in the capacity of Inspiration, that the little spark
not only appears within him but that it now shines out in a
mighty flaming strength of thinking through which he
experiences something that shows itself to be utterly related
to, and yet utterly independent of, his inner being. This is
because he has observed his activity as being not only internal
but also as being practised externally. Thus even here in this
mystical remnant there is something which is mere knowledge of what is within while also being knowledge of what is
connected with the external world.

And now we come to work which is the opposite of the
work of the mystic. We now have to do something which
resembles ordinary scientific work, for we must go out into
the external world. The latter is what is difficult, but it is
necessary if Intuitive knowing is to come about. The person
must now turn his attention away from his own activity, he
must forget what he has been doing in order to bring the Rose
Cross into being. If he is patient, if he carries out his exercises

long enough and correctly, then he will see that something remains for him about which he is certain that it is absolutely independent of his own inner experiences. It is not subjectively tinged; it leads him upwards to something which is independent of his subjective personality; and yet through his objective being it shows that it is identical with something that is the centre of his own being: the human I. In order to attain Intuitive knowing one goes out of oneself and yet arrives at something that is identical with one's own inner being. In this way we rise up from what we experience inwardly to that which is spiritual, which we now experience not in our inner being but in the external world.

In a rather primitive way very many anthroposophists interpret this matter by, for example, drawing a picture on the blackboard to illustrate what is meant by the teachings about the Rose Cross.[17] And these pictures then turn up everywhere in the group meetings. In this way what is felt inwardly and what is intended inwardly becomes fixed externally. Usually I deal with these 'artistic endeavours' by not looking at them in the group meetings. They are primitive and not very enlightening, but in addition they are misguided attempts to depict what is intended to come across spiritually by word of mouth as a teaching which is then given some kind of artistic aspect. This is nonsense. You cannot transfer into a work of art what is intended as a teaching.

3. The Rose Cross Meditation in *Occult Science, An Outline*—Further Suggestions as to Method

Meditation for Imagination; Phase I, pp. 72-80

Elevation to a supersensible state of consciousness can only come about on the basis of ordinary daytime consciousness in which the soul lives before setting out on its ascent.[18] The schooling gives the soul the means by which it can transcend this daytime consciousness, but initially the method we shall discuss still relates to ordinary daytime consciousness. The most meaningful methods are those that consist in calm and quiet activities in which the soul involves itself through specific thought-pictures which have the power to awaken certain hidden capacities of the human soul. They differ from everyday thought-pictures, which have the purpose of picturing external things. However, the thought-pictures in question do not have the aim of leading the pupil directly towards a spiritual schooling. In not depicting anything external it is their aim to have an awakening effect on the soul. The best thought-pictures are those that have a *symbolic* content. Others, though, can also be used, for the actual content is not at all relevant. What matters is that the soul concentrates all its power on having nothing in its consciousness other than the chosen thought-picture.

Whereas in ordinary life the soul's attention is directed to many things with rapidly changing thought-pictures, for spiritual schooling it is necessary to concentrate all the forces of the soul on one thought-picture. And this thought-picture must be placed by an act of will at the very centre of the pupil's consciousness. That is why symbols are better than thought-pictures which portray points of reference from the external world, for with these the soul is less self-contained than it is in the case of symbols brought into being by its own energy. It is not a matter of *what* is depicted. The important thing is that the manner in which the thought-picture is created should free the soul from any dependence on the physical world.

One can reach an understanding of what this absorption in a thought-picture implies by first considering *the concept of memory*. If one looks at a tree, for example, and then looks elsewhere, so that one no longer sees it, one can nonetheless still retain a thought-picture of the tree in one's mind. This thought-picture one has when one no longer sees something with one's eyes is a *memory* of the tree. So now suppose one retains this memory in one's soul; one allows the soul to rest upon the memory-picture while endeavouring to exclude all other thought-pictures. One's soul is thus *immersed* in the memory-picture of the tree which is, however, a memory-picture of something one has perceived with one's senses. If, though, one does the same with a memory-picture placed in one's consciousness by an act of free will, then one will gradually be able to reach the required effect.

Let us now consider an example of our soul becoming immersed in a symbolic thought-picture. First of all this calls for a symbolic picture to be developed in the soul, and this can be done in the following way. Imagine a plant rooted in the soil and bringing forth one leaf after another before finally unfolding its flower. And then imagine a human being standing beside the plant. The thought must be developed in the soul that a human being possesses characteristics and abilities that are rather more perfect than those of the plant, and that he can move from one place to another in accordance with his feelings and his wishes, whereas the plant is firmly rooted in the soil.

And now one has to say to oneself: Well, the human being is indeed more perfect than the plant; but he also has certain characteristics which are not evident in the plant, and the absence of these makes the plant appear more perfect to me than does the human being. The human being is filled with urges and passions, and it is in accordance with these that he behaves. In connection with the human being I can see that he may act in accordance with those desires and passions, whereas in the case of the plant I can see how it follows the pure laws of growth, putting forth one leaf after another and turning its flower towards the chaste rays of the sun without any passion. So I can say to myself: The human being is in a certain degree of perfection more advanced than the plant; but he has acquired this perfection by adding to what appear to me to be the chaste forces of the plant other forces, namely those desires, lusts and passions.

I then consider how the green sap flows through the plant and how this is an expression of a pure law of growth which is devoid of passion. And I further consider how it is red blood that flows through the human being's veins and how this is an expression of his urges, desires and passions. All this I consider in lively thoughts in my soul. And then I continue with further thoughts by imagining how the human being is capable of developing, and how through the higher capacities of his soul he is capable of chastening and purifying his urges and passions. I imagine how this annihilates the baseness of these urges and passions, allowing them to be reborn at a higher level.

Thus it becomes justifiable to see the blood as an expression of the purified and chastened urges and passions. So now I can look in spirit at, for example, the rose and say to myself: In the red juices of the rose I see the green colour of the plant's sap transformed into that red; and just like the green leaf, the red rose follows the chaste passionless laws of growth. So the red rose can become for me a symbol of blood expressing purified urges and passions that have cast off everything base and in their purity resemble the forces that are at work in the red rose.

I now endeavour to allow such thoughts to come alive not only in my intellect but in my feelings. I can have a blissful feeling when I imagine the growing plant, pure and passionless; I can generate the feeling in myself of how certain higher perfections have to be purchased by means of acquiring the urges and the desires. This can then transform the bliss I felt earlier into an earnest feeling; and then a feeling of liberating joy can begin to stir in me when I turn to the thought of the red blood which can become the bearer of inner experiences that are as pure as the red juices of the rose. It all comes down to not being without feeling when one builds up a symbolic thought-picture.

After working with thoughts and feelings of this kind one can turn to transforming them into the following symbolic image. One can imagine a black cross; this is to be a *symbol* representing the now annihilated lower nature of the urges and passions; and at the point where the two bars cut across one another one now imagines the seven red, shining roses arranged in a circle.

These roses are to be the *symbol* for the blood which now represents the cleansed and purified passions and urges.[*]

A symbolic thought-picture of this kind is to be developed in the soul in the same way as a memory. If one immerses oneself inwardly in a thought-picture such as this it has the power to awaken the soul. While being thus immersed one must seek to exclude any other thought-picture. Solely the symbol must appear before the soul as vibrantly as possible. It is significant that this symbol has not been presented here merely as being an awakening thought-picture but rather that it was initially developed via certain thought-pictures of the plant and the human being. The effectiveness of a symbol such as this depends on it having first been developed in the manner described before one immerses oneself in it. If one places it before one's soul without having first carried out the build-up in one's soul in the manner described, it remains cold and is much less effective as an illuminating force in the soul than when it is properly prepared.

---

[*] It is of no consequence whether or not the above thoughts can be justified by science. The important thing is to develop thoughts like this concerning the plant and the human being without any reference to theory but simply by contemplating them directly. Such thoughts are meaningful in their own right, quite apart from any other more theoretical but no less significant connections regarding their relationship with the external world. Here the thoughts are not aimed at making scientific statements, for their purpose is to build up a symbol which proves effective in the soul regardless of what might occur to one person or another while the symbol is in the process of being developed.

While immersed in the symbol, one must not pay any attention to all the preparatory thoughts out of which it has emerged. The symbol alone must stand before the soul, and one must allow the *feeling* to accompany it which came into being as a result of those preparatory thoughts. The effectiveness arises from the sojourn of the soul in this experience. And the longer the sojourn can be maintained without interference from other distracting thoughts, the more effective will the overall process be. Apart from the period of the actual contemplation, however, it is good to go repeatedly through the thoughts and feelings experienced during the build-up in order to prevent the feeling from fading away. The greater the patience applied to this renewal, the more significant will the image be for the soul. (The descriptions in my book *Knowledge of the Higher Worlds* include further examples of how one can approach inner contemplation. Especially effective are the meditations described there about the coming into being and dying away of a plant, about the forces of the future slumbering in the seed of a plant, about the formation of crystals, and so on. The intention here in the present book has been to give an example of the essence of meditation.)

A symbol such as the one described here does not depict any external thing or being brought into existence by nature. This is the very reason why it possesses the power to awaken certain capacities that belong only to the soul. Of course someone might voice an objection to this. He might say: 'Certainly, the "whole thing" as a symbol does not exist in nature; but all the details have been derived from nature—the black colour, the roses, and so on, all these things are perceived by the senses.' Well, those who are troubled by an objection like this should consider that it is not the images of the sense perceptions which lead to the awakening of higher soul faculties. What brings this about is simply the way in which the details are *brought together*. This bringing together *per se* does not result in an image of something existing in the sense-perceptible world.

A symbolic picture is here taken as an example to illustrate how the process of contemplation comes about in the soul. For the purpose of spiritual schooling all kinds of images of this kind can be used, and they can be assembled in many different ways. Certain sentences, formulae, even single words, may be used into which one is to immerse oneself. In every instance the aim of these means of inner contemplation will be to wrest the soul away from sense perceptions and bring about an activity the impression of which is meaningless for the physical senses but which brings about the awakening of slumbering capacities of soul.

There can indeed also be contemplation within feelings, within sensations and so on, which can be especially effective. Take the sensation of joy. In normal life the soul can experience joy when an external incentive for joy is present. When a healthy soul perceives how an individual does something arising from his kindness of heart, it will rejoice at such an action. And the soul may then ponder over a deed of this kind. It might say: A deed which is carried out in goodness of heart is one in which the doer does not follow his own interests but rather those of his fellows. A deed of this kind is what one calls 'a good deed'. But the soul in contemplation can free itself entirely from the idea of this individual case in the external world which gave it pleasure or delight, so that it then contemplates the overall idea of goodness of heart. It can then think how goodness of heart arises when one soul absorbs the interests of another and makes them its own. And the soul can then experience joy over the moral idea of goodness of heart. This is joy not about a process in the world of the senses; it is joy about an *idea* as such. When one endeavours to hold joy of this kind in the soul for a longer period of time, this is contemplation in a feeling. It is then not the idea which awakens the inner soul faculties but rather the prolonged acceptance by the soul of a feeling which has not been brought about by an external impression.

Because supersensible knowing is able to penetrate more deeply into the essence of things than is ordinary thinking, it can lead to feelings which work in an even more lofty degree when they are applied to inner contemplation. Since such contemplation is necessary for higher degrees of schooling, one should take into account that an energetic contemplation within feelings, such as those engendered for example by contemplating goodness of heart, can bring about considerable progress.

Since people differ in their nature, the methods of schooling they find helpful will vary. And as far as the duration of a contemplation is concerned, one should remember that the more calm and serene it is, the greater will be its effect. One should, though, avoid any exaggeration. A certain inner rhythm arising out of the exercise itself can teach the pupil what is best in this respect.

As a rule the pupil will find that he will need to practise

contemplation in this way for quite some time before being able to notice any effect. Patience and perseverance are very much a part of spiritual schooling. Those who do not bring these to life within themselves, thus quietly continuing with their exercises with patience and perseverance as their fundamental mood of soul, will make little progress.

It will be clear from what has been described so far that inner contemplation (meditation) is a means by which knowledge of higher worlds can be attained; but it will also be clear that not just any kind of content of the meditation is suitable. It must be a content which has been built up in the manner described.

Now, exercises for Inspiration and Intuition, present.

Cognition through Inspiration and Intuition can also only be attained through exercises in the realm of soul and spirit.[19] These are similar to those of 'inner contemplation' (meditation) given for the attainment of Imagination. Whereas the exercises that lead to Imagination are associated with impressions derived from the sense-perceptible physical world, these must be increasingly eliminated with regard to exercises leading to Inspiration. In order to gain an idea of what is necessary, let us turn once more to the symbol of the Rose Cross. By immersing oneself in this, one sees a picture of which the parts have been derived from the sense-perceptible world: the black colour of the cross, the roses, and so on. However, the compilation of these parts of the Rose Cross has not been derived from the sense-perceptible, physical world.

So now, if the pupil of the spirit seeks to banish entirely from his consciousness both the black cross and the red roses, as images of sense-perceptible things, while at the same time retaining in his soul the spiritual activity which brought those parts together, then he will have a resource which will lead gradually to Inspiration.

Looking into his own soul the pupil must ask himself: 'What did I do inwardly in order to combine cross and rose in that symbol? I want to come to grips with what I did (with the process in my own soul). But I want to banish the picture as such from my consciousness. I want to *feel* within me what my soul did in order to create the image; but I do not want to see before me the image itself. I now want to live inwardly in my own activity which created the image. I want to immerse myself not in a picture but in the activity of my own soul which created it.'

This is the kind of immersion that must be undertaken with regard to many symbols. This then leads to knowledge through Inspiration. Here is another example. One might contemplate the image of a plant beginning to grow and then dying away. One allows the image to grow in one's soul of a plant coming into being; it sprouts from the seed, it unfolds one leaf after another right up to the flower and the fruit. And then one imagines how it begins to wither and finally die. Gradually, by immersing oneself in a picture of this kind, one arrives at a feeling of coming into being and dying away, of which the plant is merely an image. Out of this feeling, if the exercise is carried out with perseverance, there can emerge the imagination of metamorphosis on which that physical coming into being and dying away is based.

But if one wants to proceed further and arrive at the corresponding inspiration, one has to tackle the exercise in a different way. One must reflect on one's own activity of soul which, out of the image of the plant, generated the idea of coming into being and dying away. One must now allow the plant to disappear entirely from one's consciousness and immerse oneself solely in what one did inwardly. It is only possible to rise to Inspiration if one carries out such exercises.

Initially it will not be easy for the pupil of the spirit to comprehend fully how he might set about tackling such an exercise. This arises from the fact that an individual who is accustomed to allowing his inner life to be entirely deter-mined by external impressions immediately becomes unsure of himself; he begins to sway and totter if he is now expected to develop another kind of soul life, one which has to discard all connection with external impressions. To an even greater degree than is necessary for acquiring imaginations, the pupil of the spirit must clearly understand in connection with these exercises for Inspiration that he should only embark on them if he can apply all the precautions necessary for ensuring that his power of judgement, his life of feeling and indeed his character are secured. If he succeeds in taking these pre-cautions he will be successful in two ways. Firstly the exer-cises will not cause him to lose the equanimity of his personality when he becomes supersensibly perceptive; and secondly he will become capable of carrying out properly what is called for by these exercises.

One will find these exercises difficult until one has devel-oped a specific mood of soul and specific feelings and sensations. But once an individual has patiently and perse-veringly developed within himself the qualities of soul favourable for the birth of supersensible cognition he will soon reach an understanding for them and an ability to carry them out. Once he has become accustomed to communing inwardly not in order to muse about himself but in order to consider and understand the experiences life has brought, the effort will be well rewarded. He will find that his ideas and feelings are enriched when one experience gained in life is considered in relation to another. He will come to realize the high degree in which one discovers something new not only through gaining new impressions and new experiences but also through allowing former impressions to work within oneself. If he allows his experiences, and even the opinions he has formed, to play upon one another as though neither he himself nor his own sympathies and antipathies, his own interests and feelings, are involved, he will find he is preparing an especially favourable basis for the faculty of supersensible cognition. He will indeed be developing what one may call a *rich inner life.* Most important in all this is the harmony and balance among the various characteristics of the soul. Especially effective are symbolic images.[20] And I want to remind you especially of one such: the profoundly mean-ingful symbol of the black cross with the roses. Let us bring before our soul the abstract meaning of this, Goethe's 'dying and becoming', namely the requirement that in developing our soul we should rise above matters of the sense-percep-tible world so that all around us it disappears, dies away. The one whose soul remains empty and void is 'but a gloomy guest on the dark earth'. If you succeed and you are entirely sure that something higher is rising up out of the hidden depths of your soul, then you will have come into being anew in higher worlds. Dying away in the cross, rising again in the roses—this is what lies in the symbol of the Rose Cross. The spirit is alive everywhere in the world of minerals and plants and one senses intuitively that the spirit underlying everything is the origin of the physical. The external world is in the final analysis the physiognomy of a world of spirit. [*general form or appearance of something*]

The human soul is like steel or flintstone; out of itself, in the human being's life of soul, it conjures forth divine, spiritual content. It is up to us to find the correct symbol. Someone might well say: 'You can have all sorts of fancies as regards the meaning of the Rose Cross.' But the researcher takes no notice. If a physicist discovers a law of nature, well— that means something to us, say the scientists; but the Rose Cross tells us nothing. But that is not the point. Symbols are at their most effective when there are many possible interpretations. We enter into a purely inward activity of soul; and by referring to the symbol as our point of departure we concentrate our soul upon this symbol.

Let us consider what the soul consciously does; that is what matters. There are at work within the human being forces which are capable of awakening something which is asleep, experiences that guarantee that something is an inner reality when the human being senses: 'Actually, the cross has merely been acting as a bridge. From it I have received something in my life of soul, something entirely different which is rising up in my soul, an experience which cannot be obtained by external means.'

Initially the pupil does not know whether he is facing a *Fata Morgana* or something real. It is now necessary to [*mirage*] develop yet more capacities, for what has been described is in itself still a detour for the clairvoyant; these are images. As the exercises continue the feeling then arises: 'All will depend upon what comes to expression in the images.'

If you press on your eyelid or stimulate your eye with an electrical impulse, a glimmer of light might result in the eye, caused by its inner configuration. This resembles what it is like when the images appear; they streak through the soul like spiritual flashes of lightning. When you encounter an object you know that it is not brought into existence by your eyes but is making itself known to them. This is the same spiritually. The seer knows in the same way that he did not create the object but that the object is brought to expression by his inner organs. In the very way in which images are experienced, so are objective facts experienced. Just as one distinguishes externally between fantasy and perception, so is it necessary for the seer to retain his healthy senses, for there is scarcely a realm other than that of inner experience in which one thing can so easily be mistaken for another. That is why something else must take place in parallel.

If the seer were to practise only what has just been described, he would become a madman who believes himself capable, through his own person, of conjuring up appearance as reality. In experiencing the higher world of spirit, it is necessary for the human being to divest himself of anything connected with his wishes and inclinations. But individuals today are inclined to behave in a different way. They may very well correct external sense impressions, but in doing so they are all too ready to allow feelings or subjective inclinations to have their say. An experience of spiritual reality must be preceded by a renunciation of every wish for something to appear in one way or another. Only when all sympathy has been eliminated can something spiritual be perceived with objectivity.

And something else is also essential. For those who are being guided along the path of clairvoyance with a professional attitude lacking in any dilettantism, so that they learn to see in a manner which reveals the truth, it is necessary that they do not set out on the path without some specific preconditions having been met. It is a difficult path. So prior to setting out they must have taken in certain truths, imparted to them by those who have already carried out some research. One can also follow the path armed with less knowledge, but then one's soul world remains impoverished; its content is held in check by fixed ideas. This is what happens with those clairvoyants who believe, for example, that they have become united with God, describing Him in such and such a way, and so on. When such clairvoyants describe the higher worlds their portrayals appear banal. But when experienced spiritual researchers enter into the higher worlds the content of those worlds appears to them in all its manifold diversity, whereas everything external proves to be nothing more than a small excerpt of those great worlds. An individual who has this experience knows that what he undergoes there is no deception. He perceives spiritually with the same assuredness as is the case in the world of the senses. This is well-schooled clairvoyance.

It is most important for the spiritual researcher who intends to direct his steps into the spiritual world that much of what becomes for others a direct understanding and aim is for him simply an educational means to an end, an intimate educational means for the soul.[21] Let me give you an example of this. Many years ago I wrote a book, *The Philosophy of Freedom*. [...] This *Philosophy of Freedom* differs greatly from other philosophical works of the present time of which the aim, more or less, is to show what things are like in the world or what, in the opinion of the author, they ought to be like. This is not the aim of my book. Its aim is to give those who enter into the thoughts it describes a kind of training in thinking so that this method of thinking, this specific method by which thoughts are approached, brings about movement in the feelings and sensations of the soul—just as gymnastics, if I may make this comparison, sets the limbs in motion.

What is otherwise merely a means for imparting knowledge is in my book also a means by which the reader can educate his own spiritual and soul life. This is exceedingly important. The book is understandably annoying for many philosophers of our day who do not connect philosophy with something that is intended to help people progress along their path in the assumption that they should retain the normal ability to think with which people are usually endowed. This book, however, is not so concerned with the question of whether one point or another is disputable, or whether something should be comprehended in one way or another, but rather with providing thoughts which can be united in a coherent whole and can school our soul and help it to progress a little further.

The same goes for my book *Truth and Science*, and also for much which intends to provide the basic elements for

[handwritten margin note:] Published 1894. He suggested the title "The Phil. of Spiritual Activity" as the title of the English translation

[handwritten note at bottom:] written 1892. Steiner said that the book "Phil. of Freedom" was written to provide the phil. foundations of "Tr. + Sc."

training the soul to find its way into the spiritual world. Mathematics and geometry teach us about triangles, squares and other figures. But why do they teach us all this? So that we may become acquainted with matters of space, what laws apply here, and so on. And the spiritual ascent into higher worlds works, basically, with similar figures as symbols. It presents the pupil with, for example, the symbol of the triangle, or the square or other figures, but in this connection not for the purpose of gaining direct knowledge, which is obvious anyway, but so that he can receive the possibility of schooling his spiritual faculties in a way which enables the spirit to use the impressions engendered by these symbols to guide him upward towards a higher world. It is a matter, then, of thought schooling or—do not misunderstand me—of thought gymnastics. In this sense much of dry-as-dust external science or dry-as-dust external philosophy, much of mathematics or geometry provides a living symbol for spiritual schooling which can lead us up into the spiritual world.

If we ponder on this in our soul we will learn to comprehend what actually no external science understands about the way in which the ancient Pythagoreans, under the influence of their great teacher Pythagoras, said about the universe as consisting of numbers, for they were able to focus on the inherent law of number. In contrast, consider how we encounter numbers everywhere in the world today. There is nothing easier than the debunking of spiritual science or anthroposophy by those who speak from what seems to be a very lofty standpoint, saying: 'Here come those spiritual scientists from their mystical obscurity with their symbolism of numbers, telling us that numbers govern inherent laws so that, for example, the true foundation of the human being is the number seven.' Well, this is indeed what Pythagoras and his pupils meant when they spoke about the inherent laws of numbers. If we allow that wonderful interrelationship between numbers to work upon our spirit, then we shall be able to train it in a way which will awaken it out of its sleep, so that it can develop greater strengths within itself in order to enter into the spiritual world.

So schooling is also possible through such other sciences. This is what is spoken about as studies for those who wish to enter into the spiritual world. For such an individual, everything can become an inner symbol which is seen by others as robust reality, or more or less an outer symbol. When an individual is able to allow these symbols to work on him he not only frees his spirit from the external, physical world but also imbues it with powerful forces, so that his soul can be aware of it even when there is no outer motivation. I have already mentioned that when someone allows a symbol such as that of the Rose Cross to work upon his soul he can gain from this an impulse to ascend into the spiritual world. When thinking of the Rose Cross we imagine a simple black cross with a circle of seven red roses attached where the two beams intersect.

What does it tell us? To allow it to work in the right way upon one's soul one may think to oneself: 'I observe, for example, a plant; I say of this plant that it is an imperfect entity. And beside it I place a human being who, in his own way, is a more perfect entity—although only in his own way. The fact is that, in contemplating the plant, I have before me an entity which is not permeated with passions, urges and instincts that would bring it down from the heights where it otherwise resides. The plant possesses its own inborn laws which it follows from leaf to flower to fruit; and there it stands, passionless and chaste. Beside it, on the other hand, lives the human being who is, certainly, in his way a higher being; but he is filled with urges, instincts and passions which can cause him to stray from the stern laws that govern him. He is obliged to overcome something within himself if he, too, wants to follow his inborn laws as does the plant.'

The human being can say to himself: 'My red blood is the expression of urges and instincts within me. I can compare this in a certain way with the chaste plant sap, the chlorophyll, which is in the red rose.' And then I can say: If the human being has become so strong within himself that the red blood is no longer an expression of all that pushes him down beneath himself but has instead become something which lifts him up; if it has become the expression of something as chaste as the red rose in which the plant's sap has become red; if, in other words, the red of the rose is an expression of chaste inwardness, the purified being of man in his blood—then that is the ideal of what the human being can achieve through overcoming his outer nature portrayed for me in the symbol of the black cross with its charred wood. And the red rose symbolizes the more exalted life which awakens when the red blood becomes a chaste expression of the human being's instinctual nature now purified.

If one does not allow this description to become an abstract idea, then it will become an idea for livingly experienced inner development. A whole world of feelings and sensibilities will come to life within us; and we will sense within us a development from a less perfect to a more perfect inner state. This development is felt to be quite different from that abstract concept described by everyday science as some purely external Darwinism. This development will cleave its way right into our heart, it will imbue us with warmth, with warmth of soul, and it will become within us a strength which bears and upholds us. Such inner experiences alone can enable the soul to develop powerful forces within itself, those powerful forces which ensure that when it withdraws from the outside world into what otherwise would be unconsciousness it can remain instead alight with consciousness.

It would of course be childishly simple to say: 'But you are recommending the idea of something imagined, of something thought up or contrived; but there is value only in ideas which are images based on something external, and an image of the Rose Cross is not based on anything external!' Well, we are not concerned here with an idea used for schooling our soul being an image based on external reality. What matters is that the idea lends strength to our soul and lures from it what lies hidden and asleep within it. If the human soul turns towards a pictorial idea of this kind, if it takes whatever it otherwise values as reality and makes pictures of it which are not arbitrarily modelled on fantasy but are based on reality, as is the symbol of the Rose Cross, then we can say: Here is an individual who is endeavouring to advance to the first stage in knowledge of the spiritual world. This is the stage of *Imaginative knowledge* which leads us up beyond what is directly involved in the physical world.

Thus someone who wishes to ascend towards the spiritual

world will work in his soul in a specific way which causes what otherwise belongs to the external world to work upon him. He himself works in his soul. After he has worked in this way for a while, scientists of the external world might well say to him: 'All this has only subjective value for you; it is purely individual.' But a scientist of the external world does not realize that through such strict, regular training a stage of development is reached in which the possibility for the soul to experience subjective feelings and sensations ceases entirely, so that it has to say to itself: 'I am now inwardly experiencing images which confront me just as otherwise trees and rocks, rivers and mountains, plants and animals of the external world confront me; these images are just as real as are those external, physical things upon which my subjectivity can have no influence whatsoever.'

So there is indeed an intermediate stage for anyone wishing to rise up to the spiritual world, a stage in which the individual is in danger of taking into the spiritual world something subjective, which is valid only for himself. However, the seeker must transcend this intermediate stage. And he will then arrive at a stage in which whatever is experienced by the soul can be just as objectively proven—for someone who is capable of comprehending this—as can any things present in external, physical reality be proven.

4. Caduceus and Rose Cross— Protective Meditations

What, initially, is our aim in meditation?[22] We must lose all awareness of ourselves by obliterating whatever has to do with ordinary life; we must immerse ourselves entirely in the words prescribed so that we no longer know or feel anything either about our body or about the thoughts and feelings of everyday life. This, however, is the very thing which the adversary powers wish to prevent! They seek to draw us back into everyday life by preventing us from concentrating our thoughts. As soon as we become aware of this happening—for example in the meditation 'In the light's pure rays...'[23]* where the intention is that we should think and feel solely about light as the garment of the Godhead while living entirely in this image—we may turn to the caduceus as an effective symbol. We think of a brightly shining yellow staff entwined by two serpents, a dark one and a shining white one, beginning with the dark one.

---

* In the light's pure rays
The Godhead of the world shines forth,
In pure love for all beings
Divinity shines into my soul,
I rest with the Godhead of the world.
I shall find myself
In the Godhead of the world.

Every living being is contained within a skin as a sign that it is enclosed within the physical world. The etheric body, too, has a skin, as does also the astral body. So when the human being receives impressions of the day via his senses, this affects the skin of his astral body; it becomes scuffed and worn, it gets torn and cracked. This manifests as tiredness. As we fall asleep this skin tears and while we sleep it is renewed. Before going to sleep, we should endeavour to become aware of this process. We can imagine how we are now entering into the spiritual worlds where in the realms of harmonies and the music of the spheres the astral body is restored by the spiritual beings. As we fall asleep we should be filled with a feeling of gratitude toward those divine beings and powers; we should have a feeling of love for wisdom. Then bad influences will be unable to approach us.

Just as the human being uses up and then renews the skin of his soul life over the course of 24 hours, so does a snake periodically slough off its skin, divesting itself of it and then renewing it. That is why viewing the caduceus in spirit is an effective means for penetrating into spiritual worlds while meditating; it overcomes inhibiting influences.

Another method is to feel oneself enfolded within a blue aura that protects us against all bad thoughts and feelings which might endeavour to approach us from the outside. We feel inwardly how this aura protects us against all base influences. Only good influences can gain entry into our soul. This may be combined effectively with the following meditation.

A meditation for protection against external influences:

The outer cloak of my aura is growing denser.
May it contain me within a vessel
Impenetrable to all impure, unchaste thoughts and feelings.
*May it open itself solely to the divine wisdom.**

A beginner will initially experience the presence of dark forces in his distracted thoughts whereas a more advanced researcher will see such astral forces as parasitic animals, as rats and mice. Well, someone seeing these rats and mice should not be pleased at having come so far without having fallen prey entirely to those forces. One has to strengthen oneself further in order to resist the influence of such dark forces.

A second typical experience can also occur during meditation. Once again the beginner senses it whereas the more advanced researcher sees it. This feels as though our physical body no longer belongs to us but is instead fragmented and distributed across the universe. Even organs such as the heart, the liver and the gall bladder dilate. In this process we remember that of course our physical body came into being on Saturn through the inflowing of substantiality belonging to the Thrones, our ether body through the Spirits of Wisdom on Old Sun, our astral body through the Spirits of Movement on Old Moon, while on earth the I was given to us by the Spirits of Form. We return to these spirits in our meditation. But one must not imagine that every organ returns to those powers which originally implanted it during the cosmic development of the world. There is, rather, a sense of merging with the ambience of those powers whereby

---

* The second line has elsewhere been noted as: '*May it surround me with an impenetrable skin.*'

we must remain consistently aware of our own I while also feeling how we belong to the spiritual powers in question.

Another typical experience during meditation is that of our consciousness growing weaker or indeed being forcibly dimmed. In a certain sense this does indeed occur, but we must constantly strive to remain alert. One aid here is the black cross with the seven red roses. This is the great symbol of Christ Jesus himself, the Rose Cross—fading, dying life which has within itself the power to engender new life from out of itself. In fact, to look in spirit at this symbol always has a strengthening effect on spiritual development; it gives strength to our daily life in every situation—for the Seducer does indeed come closest to us when we are involved in spiritual exercises. The more advanced researcher sees this exactly as it is described in the Bible.

Finally, as we continue with our meditation, a feeling of profound peace arises in our soul; not an external feeling of quietness but a profoundly inward sense of peace which nothing can disturb however great the uproar and clamour surrounding us may be.

These are the three typical phenomena that occur as we meditate, among many others which vary depending upon the individuality of the one who meditates:

1. Phenomena of temptation (parasitic animals).
2. Being distributed among the various hierarchies, whereby we must not allow ourselves to lose our I-consciousness (Rose Cross).
3. Being granted the most profound peace of soul possible.*

---

*Another record adds: '1. Disturbance through inimical powers. 2. Weakening of consciousness. 3. Peace of soul.'

The caduceus assists us in entering into the spiritual worlds while the Rose Cross confirms us in this.

There are two eventualities we must endeavour to avoid entirely during our spiritual schooling. We must never cause harm to anyone either in deed, thought or word, nor by making the excuse of not having intended any harm; it is irrelevant whether we have acted intentionally or not. The second is that a sensation of hatred must be expunged utterly from our feeling life, for otherwise it re-emerges as a feeling of fear; for fear is suppressed hatred. We must transform hatred into a feeling of love, of love for wisdom.

A means exists whereby we can prevent the ahrimanic beings from entering into our consciousness, a symbol to be brought to life within us.[24] This is the staff of Mercury, the caduceus, the shining rod entwined by a black snake and a brightly shimmering snake. A snake symbolizes the astral body. The astral body sloughs off its skin every evening, discarding the worn-out husk. This is symbolized by the black snake. During the night it receives a new, sparkling skin, and this newly alive, beautiful iridescent skin of the astral body is symbolized by the shimmering snake.

 If we bring it to life within us prior to any meditation, this symbol will banish whatever disturbance wants to enter into our consciousness: the caduceus held aloft by the herald of the gods, showing the way. When the researcher makes progress and becomes clairvoyant, the ahrimanic beings press in upon him in images. He sees parasitic animals, rats and mice. Temptations in the form of beings approach him, with beautiful human faces but deformed feet. One must not fall prey to such images. Good images are those when the one who meditates sees a sphinx (seraph) or a cherub. Even here the caduceus is used to ward off beings that drag him down.

When he makes upward progress, the new exercises bring about a sense of being divided up or of melting away. These sensations are quite justified. Here the human being is the dismembered Dionysus. But he must not lose his awareness. To understand this we must realize the following. On Saturn, the Thrones, those lofty, sublime beings, worked on the physical body. The physical body does not belong to us; it is an optical illusion. Currents streaming from the lofty Thrones form it. Imagine streams of water flowing; where they meet a whirlpool arises. In the same way the physical arises where the streams of the Thrones meet. The physical body is something lofty, something hallowed at which the Thrones are still working. The ether body was formed on Old Sun by the Spirits of Wisdom. And on Old Moon the Spirits of Movement worked on creating the astral body. On earth the Spirits of Form are at work on the I.

Thus the sensation of melting away is entirely justified. We feel as though we are being given back to the streams which formed us. But this is where the lower beings endeavour to extinguish the meditant's consciousness, and this must not be permitted to happen. In order to prevent it, whenever one notices one's consciousness dwindling one may place the Rose Cross before one's soul. It is also very good to contemplate this at the close of every exercise. Before the exercise stands the caduceus, and at the end the Rose Cross. One imagines the black cross to represent whatever is base or animal-like in the human being; and from it must sprout the seven red roses.

A beautiful legend tells: As Christ was hanging on the cross with bleeding wounds, bees came and sucked honey from them just as they do with red roses. The sacrifice had caused the chemical constituents of the blood to be transformed so that it became as pure as the sap of the red roses.

The next stage on the path is when we rediscover ourselves consciously in the higher spheres. There we do not feel ourselves to be an I, for we are now entirely selfless. And then the following temptation occurs. The devil shows us the world which now appears to the meditant with a degree of splendour. He says: 'Look, there is the world. It shall belong to you if you become my follower.' Everything personal must now be extinguished, and at that moment one finds that one's I shines out in consciousness. In order to resist the temptations of the devil one can meditate on the Rose Cross.

Having now rediscovered ourselves consciously in the meditation, we feel around us the region of peace of soul. But there is more than peace alone in this region. In it the battle of the gods also rages; thunder rampages in ways of which our earthly battles are merely feeble imitations. Peace within the battle—just as in water the same substance can contain both quietness and storms. The following is scarcely possible for present-day human beings. But if it were possible the image would be of standing on a sinking ship knowing that in a moment one would be meeting physical death while at the same time feeling intoxicated by the beauty of raging nature and thus blissfully awaiting death.

Thus the meditant rests in the region of peace of soul, in blissful peace while being aware of the storm and battle raging in that same region.

One great obstacle for the meditant is hatred which lacerates the astral body and causes putrefaction in the physical body leading to deathly vibrations within it. The human being is just as responsible for unintentional damage as he is for intentional damage done to others. If one merely represses hatred its vibrations are transformed into fear. An individual who is fearful can never embark on esoteric research because he still bears repressed hatred within himself. One must endeavour to avoid unintentionally causing hurt next time. It is much easier to harbour good intentions than it is to act wisely. One must acquire love of wisdom within oneself in order to transform hatred. This love of wisdom flows from the theosophical world view. [...]

When the meditant succeeds in entering into the realm of the spirit his astral body expands; he has left his outer casing and now has a sensation of being divided up. He no longer feels he is a self-contained entity and he has forgotten his earthly, personal name. This is necessary and is worth striving for; but there is some danger in it. If he then loses his awareness and becomes unconscious or falls into a trance, this weakens him. He is then at the mercy of mediumistic influences which are harmful. If he senses that this state is coming upon him, he should turn the eyes of his soul to the Rose Cross, the cross with the roses. First he imagines it, and subsequently he actually sees it. This enables him to remain in his waking consciousness.

In order to attain higher knowledge, an individual must initially do something about creating higher organs for himself.[25] He must cause a world which is higher than that of ordinary reasoning to come to rest in him, and this is done by carrying out a new activity. You can easily understand that it is impossible to attain higher knowledge by means of one's ordinary consciousness. [...] The individual must therefore do something towards creating a new activity within himself which can confront the world of archetypes and bring it to a standstill. He does this by learning, for example, to find his way through inner experiences which do not belong among the experiences of his ordinary consciousness. One such experience is described in my book *Occult Science* where the building up of the Rose Cross image is described.

How should one proceed in order to experience this image of the Rose Cross inwardly in the right way? Although this has already been described here in Vienna, I will describe it again today as a part of the overall picture we now need to create. Someone whose task it is to lead a pupil of the spirit to higher stages of knowledge, initially by making a small step at the beginning, would be obliged to say: 'Watch how a plant grows up out of the soil. You can see how leaf grows after leaf until the flower and then the fruit is reached. You can see as it grows that it is filled with the green plant sap.' And now we compare this plant with the human being. We know that the human being is filled with what we call blood, and we also know that this blood provides an outward expression of the passions, urges and desires pulsing through him.

Because the human being possesses an I, he appears to us to be a higher being in comparison with the plant. Only a fantasist—and there are many—will believe that the plant possesses a consciousness like that of a human being, inwardly picturing external impressions. We do not possess consciousness on account of carrying out some activity or other—which is what the plant, too, can do—but rather because we are able inwardly to mirror external impressions. This is something of which the human being is capable. He has in a certain sense developed to a higher degree than the plant, which is not capable of this. But on account of having developed to a higher degree the human being has had to accept a certain degree of degradation, namely that he is capable of error.

The plant does not make mistakes because it follows its own laws. Here one cannot talk of error. The plant also does not possess a higher and a lower aspect; it does not have urges, desires and passions pulling it down to a lower level. Faced with a plant we can be impressed by its chastity in contrast to the human being who is filled with urges, desires and passions. Thus, in comparison with the plant, the human being with his red blood has developed to a higher degree while having to accept that for this higher development he has had to take on board a step downwards, a kind of degradation.

The teacher will explain all this to the pupil of the spirit. And then he will have to point out that the human being must attain by his own effort what appears to him in the plant at a lower level. The human being must master his urges, desires and passions which find expression in the blood surging through his veins. He will have achieved this when his higher nature conquers his lower nature, when his red blood has become as chaste as the green sap of the plant that turns red in the red rose.

In this sense the red rose can become for us a symbol of what the human being must become as he strives towards his true ideal which is fulfilled when his higher nature masters his lower nature. We look upon the rose as an example, a symbol of the purified, chastened blood. And when we unite the red rose with the black wooden cross, with its dead wood left over by the plant when it dies and withers, then the wreath of red roses upon the black wooden cross becomes a symbol of the victory of the human being's higher nature, his chastened nature, over his lower nature which he has to overcome. In the black wooden cross we have a symbol of the human being's lower nature, now overcome, and in the red rose we have the symbol of the chastened red blood.

Thus the Rose Cross is a symbol of the human being's development as it comes about in the world. The Rose Cross is not an abstract concept but a symbol of something we can sense and feel; we can grow warm in our soul when we look at the evolution of the human being as depicted in the Rose Cross.

In this we are shown that the human being can have ideas which have no external connection. Someone who wants to remain within his ordinary consciousness may well say: 'You are a fantasist! How can this Rose Cross be of any assistance?

Ideas are not true if they do not depict something external. So now you have created this Rose Cross for yourself. Where can such a thing be found? Where do red roses grow upon withered wood?'

These are remarks someone might well make. But actually the whole point is that we acquire capacities in our soul which are not yet present in normal consciousness. We must strive for an inner activity that enables us to imagine something which is not external but which can nevertheless be related to the external world even when it is not an actual picture belonging to that world. The Rose Cross has some connection with the external world, yet it is we who have created within ourselves the way in which it is thus connected. We have sensed the ascent from the plant to the human being and then the human being's further ascent. We paint the Rose Cross livingly within our imagination. And our soul might also contemplate many other such images.

So that we may understand one another more clearly I would also like to present you with another such symbol. Let us turn our attention to ordinary human life as it is lived by people as the days go by. First we notice the alternation between day and night, between waking and sleeping. During the day we have one experience after another; from morning to evening we experience all kinds of things. So then we can ask: What is it that takes place during the night? As we know from various lectures, there are certain forces from the spiritual world which are brought to us without our knowing about it. Just as during the day we have experiences of which we are conscious, so do we during the night have experiences of which we are not conscious. These things alternate.

If, then, for the purpose of some degree of self-knowledge, we turn to our inner life, we can ask: 'What kind of progress have I been making? Has every daytime experience really taken me a step further?' Does the human being have good reason to be satisfied with himself if he only moves forward just a small fraction through his daytime experiences which lead to some forces being given to him during the night? Actually, a good deal must be experienced by the human being during the day if those experiences are to add even a small degree to his maturity. If we ask ourselves how much we have gained in maturity through allowing the experiences of one day to work on us by day and thereafter the resulting forces by night, we will find that the progress of our real being, our I, is rather slow, since we allow a great many experiences to pass us by unnoticed.

We can imagine how we experience a day and make progress in our inner being somewhat like this. Perhaps we have taken a small step forward after one day, and another small step the next day, and so on. However, this is a considerable exaggeration, for many individuals scarcely move forward at all from one day to the next. If we look back over the most favourable period of our life, our childhood, we will see how rapidly the human being moves forward during childhood compared with what takes place later on in life. It is not unreasonable to claim that a globetrotter, in all he has learned throughout his worldwide travels, does not progress as much as does a child through what he learns from his nurse.

Caduceus

By means of a drawing we can depict how the I moves forward in stages. The vertical stave shows the progress, while the line weaving round it shows the daytime experiences. We have many experiences during the day, but they bring us only this far [point of intersection]. Then, during the next day, we again have many experiences which again take us a little further. And now, if we take the forces which influence us during the night, we can depict these by means of the dotted line. Thus we can depict the degree of progress made by the human being in relation to his experiences by means of a stave with two snakes, a bright one and a dark one, winding their way up it. The bright snake would depict the daytime experiences and the dark one the night-time forces. This is something like a symbol for the life of a human being.

We can create both complicated and simple symbols for ourselves. A very simple one would show a plant growing upwards to the point where it bears fruit and from then onwards withers away until everything has disappeared except its seeds. Here is how we can show in a simple symbol how a plant develops upwards and then withers away. This line would be a simple symbol for what takes place in the growing and withering plant.

In the Rose Cross we have a symbol of the human being's development from a lower to a higher stage, and in the caduceus we have a symbol of the progress made by the I through experiences during the day and during the night. We could in this way develop one symbol after another. These symbols do not represent anything external, but when we dedicate ourselves to becoming inwardly immersed in their meaning, which represents nothing external, then we shall be working in our soul in a way that will accustom it to inner activity which it otherwise does not practise. And in combination these inner activities generate a kind of inner strength that enables us to recover what we have called the world of archetypal images.

Such symbols need not only involve pictures which one can see; they can also consist of words in which profound world truths are combined. Great, all-embracing world truths expressed in symbolic words also give us material with which we can bring structure to our soul. By working on himself in this way, the human being consciously brings about what is otherwise brought about in him by the external world when his brain is formed out of the world of reason, his nervous system out of the spiritual world, and his sense organs out of the elementary world. The human being himself forms the organs that are higher than his brain and invisible externally because they lie outside the physical world. These organs are not perceptible to ordinary, every-day consciousness. Just as the eyes are formed out of the elementary world, the nervous system out of the spiritual world and the brain out of the world of reason, so are the higher sense organs—those which little by little enable us to look into spiritual worlds—formed out of the world of archetypal images. Because they come into being like spiritual flowers sprouting forth from the human being, these sense organs are known as lotus blossoms, or also spiritual wheels or chakras.

Thus for those who practise the exercises described, new

organs can become visible in clairvoyant vision, organs which cannot be perceived with ordinary consciousness. Something resembling a wheel, or a burgeoning flower, can form in the centre of the forehead; we call this the two-petalled lotus blossom. The two-petalled lotus blossom is like a spiritual sense organ. Just as our physical organs exist in order to make us aware of the physical world around us, so do the spiritual organs exist in order to make us aware of the world which we cannot see with our ordinary, everyday consciousness.

Actually, these organs are formed by forces and force-systems emanating from the human being's soul. A second lotus blossom is formed in the region of the larynx, and a third in the vicinity of the heart, and so on. We form such spiritual sense organs—a contradictory expression for which, however, our present language moulded on the physical, sense-perceptible world has no equivalent—by patiently and energetically filling our soul with symbolic images that depict nothing external. In a way that differs from ordinary conscious experiences these work in our soul and call up forces there which make a stand against the world of archetypal images.

To proceed only thus far, however, is insufficient, for we are not yet able to perceive anything. Someone who is already clairvoyant can see the sense organs which an individual has developed. But those higher sense organs must develop further if clairvoyant vision is to become possible for that individual. As yet, the organs have been formed out of a higher world, out of those worlds by which we are created. So now comes the second act by means of which actual spiritual seeing is prepared. To prepare for actual spiritual seeing, the

I Imagination

one who has attained the development of Imaginative perception, in other words the development of the lotus
blossoms, must make the transition to a higher stage of inner
soul work.

This is somewhat more difficult than the first stage. In the
first stage the pupil must create within himself as many
symbolic images as possible, symbolic images which can be
given by every present-day school of spiritual research in a
form suitable for the individual pupil. Gradually, with
patience and persistence, he then develops his spiritual sense
organs.

At the next stage, having developed a degree of proficiency
in picturing such images, the pupil then learns how to banish
them from his consciousness in order to concentrate solely
upon what they have brought into existence within him. As
you know, we developed a degree of activity within ourselves
when forming the image of the Rose Cross. We observed the
plant and we observed the human being and we looked into a
far distant future and only then were we able to create,
through the strength of our soul, that initial symbol within
ourselves. So now we allow that initial symbol to disappear
entirely. We remove the Rose Cross, or even the caduceus,
from our consciousness and ask ourselves: 'How did we
arrive at those images in the first place?' We must look at our
own activity and not at the product of that activity! This is
more difficult.

II Inspiration

We now disregard the symbols and pay attention instead to
the activity that created them. One turns one's attention to
the attention as such. Having created a symbol, one then
thinks: 'How did I do this?' One imagines what one did in

order to make it happen. Most individuals will be obliged to make many, many attempts in order to move on from the symbol to the creative activity which created it. One must become accustomed to saying to oneself: 'When I remove the symbol there is nothing left.' This will take a very, very long time. One will be obliged again and again to create the symbols in order then to relinquish one's hold on them so that an experience of the activity itself, which created those symbols, can arise.

After working on the exercises for quite some time, so that one begins to feel a bubbling and swirling within oneself, one will have reached the moment when one becomes aware not only of possessing higher organs, lotus blossoms, but also of seeing all kinds of entirely new experiences flashing up, experiences of an initial glimpse into the spiritual world. One has arrived at the stage where there is a new range of vision.

The experience is something like the following. Having left everything behind, having departed from the sense-perceptible world to which one is accustomed, and having immersed oneself in a realm of symbols, one then does away with those symbols and is surrounded by nothing but black darkness. But consciousness is not suspended, for it now bubbles and swirls with its own activity. And this now makes one capable of suspending something else in addition. Previously one suspended the world of archetypes; now one suspends something else, namely the world of reason, but in a different way—from the opposite direction. One suspends what otherwise flows in. Formerly one saw only the shadow images of the world of reason in the activity of one's own reasoning. But now one sees the world of reason from the

Cosmic Intelligence came from St. Michael. But, since the "consciousness age", this cosmic intelligence has been put into the hands of humans. Ego = sharp 2-edged sword—can be used for selfish or non-selfish reasons. started during Renaissance (1450's)

other side; now one sees those beings whom we have termed the hierarchies; now, by degrees, everything comes alive.

This, then, is the next step to be taken. But it is not yet the final one. In a further step one has to stand back also from this activity, which is one's own. First one suppressed the images and retained one's own activity. But now one must also be capable of abstaining from one's own activity, one must be capable of suppressing it. And this is when a person really working on these endeavours will notice how difficult they are. It will take a long time before he reaches any result. On the whole, when he now desists from his efforts he is likely to fall asleep or enter into a sleeplike state. But if he does succeed in retaining his consciousness, so that he can consciously suppress his activity, then he will have reached the stage at which he holds back not only his rationality but also the spiritual world. In consequence he then sees the spiritual world from the other side. He now sees, in the spiritual world, the spiritual facts and beings.

Whereas the knowledge attained by suppressing the images and retaining the activity is termed Inspired knowledge, the knowledge reached by suppressing one's activity is termed Intuitive knowledge. Through Intuitive knowledge one gains insight into the true shape of the spiritual world which is otherwise perceived only via its shadow images present in the laws of nature. Now the beings and activities that manifest in the laws and facts of nature are present in one's own field of consciousness.

You see, then, that we have thus described a process of knowledge which is different from simply bringing to a person's consciousness an immersion within oneself or a stepping-out into the spiritual world. Through the method of spiritual development described here, the individual enters into the spiritual world in an entirely different way. This method leads to the creation of organs by means of suppressing the world of archetypal images and then using it for the creation of the organs. Then, via the world of Imagination and Inspiration, the individual is led back into the spiritual world which he is now able to observe. Having progressed to the stage of Intuitive knowledge he can then develop this further, and thus be able to re-enter the elementary world of his own volition. He can then grow into it in a manner for which, instead of being unprepared, he is fully prepared because he sees this elementary world before him as the ultimate.

For many individuals, however, this is a difficult path because it calls for a high degree of self-denial. Initially the individual has to practise with the symbols for a long time, waiting for the necessary organs to be formed. And with these he can initially see nothing. Yet people nowadays are much inclined to say: 'What I want is to be able to see something!' They do not want to follow a safe path, for what they want is success. Well, success does come with this path, but it does involve a degree of self-denial.

First one has to work upon oneself in order, having done this work upon oneself, to proceed step by step along the path in the manner described until one can enter into the higher worlds. And what one initially encounters of the world of reason and the spiritual world is indeed rather colourless. Not until one has returned from the world of reason and entered into the elementary world, when one has made much progress in Intuitive knowledge, does everything shine out in full colour through being permeated by the effects of the elementary world. Only then can one describe it vividly; vivid description is only possible from the viewpoint of Intuitive knowledge.

All this calls for a degree of self-denial. Only once one has enjoyed working with the symbols and has worked further with patience and perseverance at the formation of the organs can one sense a degree of progress, although even then one still sees little of the spiritual world. But by entering with enjoyment into this inner work one supersedes the sense of self-denial. One must generate a degree of satisfaction in the subtle execution of such effort. But the reward comes relatively late. Nevertheless, it is a secure path, a path which protects one against any kind of fantasizing and any kind of illusion. Once one has worked one's way up to Imaginative knowledge one is already within that world which is directly above our own, but one only perceives this through sensing that one has absorbed into oneself something of a higher world.

Only gradually does one come to a proper comprehension of the higher worlds. In my book *Knowledge of the Higher Worlds* and in the second part of *Occult Science* you will find a sketch of the path of development leading towards the higher worlds. These things are described there, but for a wider readership so that some elements are explained more briefly. My purpose today was to go more intimately into certain aspects. You will gain a more profound understanding of these things if you combine what has been presented today with what those books depict. [...]

We have seen that the path of development described can be trodden in full consciousness. A teacher is no longer needed in the manner of older methods, where the teacher or guide relieved the pupil of certain things or gave him others, so that the one being led was not independent. Today we have been speaking about a path that is genuinely fitting for modern consciousness. Someone following this path today does not entrust himself to a spiritual teacher any more than one entrusts oneself to, say, a mathematics teacher. Of course one assumes that the teacher knows more, for if this were not the case what would be the point of approaching him? In the same sense one entrusts oneself to a teacher who simply gives certain instructions, a symbol, for example. One then notices what the effect of this symbol is. With every step one remains one's own master. One follows the instructions of the spiritual teacher in the same way as one follows the instructions of a mathematics teacher. He sets tasks, but whereas a mathematical problem is solved by means of the intellect, one's entire soul is devoted to the task set by a spiritual teacher. The whole essence of the new method of initiation shows that individual independence is fully respected so that a guru is no longer a guru in the old sense but simply a guide who gives advice such as: 'This is what you can do in order to proceed in such and such a way.'

As one age follows another in stages, so must human beings pass through one stage after another. The methods of initiation have to change. Former ages needed Initiation methods which differed from those of today. People today need the method I have been describing. It is named the Rosicrucian schooling after its most important symbol.

There are many symbols, but the Rose Cross is the most important because it is the symbol of human development. This Rosicrucian method is the most modern method of initiation which is capable today of leading us in the proper way into the higher worlds.

5. The Rose Cross Meditation with Mantric Verses Given to Individual Pupils

"Let Love Be My Guide"

Evening:

Review 5–6 minutes[26]

In the beginning was the Word
And may the Word be in me
And may the Word work in me
And may the Word bear me
Into spirit worlds
Into soul depths.

Morning:

Mental image of the Rose Cross

Be for me an image
   Of my Self.
In depths of my soul
Strong spirit forces
Like bright rose stars
Upon black wood of cross.

Evening:

Review 4–6 minutes[27]

Mental image of the Rose Cross

Seven bright rose-stars
Upon cross's black wood
   Be for me the image
Powerful forces of spirit-light
   In darkness of soul
Seek, O my soul,
In the darkness the light
                    (Quietness of soul)

Morning:

Sunlight pulsating through space
Spirit-light pulsating through the soul.

6 exercises.

Evening:

Mental image of the Rose Cross[28]

O my soul,
See this symbol:
May it express for you
The World Spirit
Who fills all space,
Who works through all time
And also works eternally in you.

(Quietness of soul)

Morning:

Mental image of the Rose Cross

May my feeling,
May my thinking,
May my will
Endure within this symbol.
May that which it betokens
Live in my heart's depths,
Live as light in me.

(Quietness of soul)

Evening:

Review. In pictures. Backwards. 5 minutes[29]

Mental image of the Rose Cross

May my soul behold
In those seven bright rose stars
Spirit power sevenfold revealed

May my soul behold
In that black wood of the cross
World darkness as light's foundations.

Be this in me
(Quietness of soul)

Morning:

Mental image of the Rose Cross

As on the black wood of the cross
Seven rose stars, shining, are revealed
May also starry light of soul reveal
Sevenfold to my deepest depths of soul:
Wisdom—Love—Certitude
Serenity—Inner peace—Courage
Holding me secure within myself
(Quietness of soul)

Subsidiary Exercises, CW 13, pp. 245–50

Evening:

I go into the world of spirit *(3 to 4 minutes)*[30]

Mental image:
  Black cross (wood transformed by fire into charcoal)
  seven roses (colour: rose-magenta)

  This symbol tells you:

  As out of the black cross
  The red roses,
  So out of the world's darkness
  The clarity of the Life of Christ.

  (Dwell within this thought for 10 minutes
  while contemplating the cross)

Morning:

  Review the events of the previous day.
  Mental image of a white cross of shining
  white sunlight—seven green roses

  As the green life
  In the white sunlight,
  So the life of Christ
  In humanity's progression.

                          (15 minutes)

  Subsidiary Exercises, CW 13, pp. 245–50

Evening:

Mental image of the Rose Cross[31]

May warmth enter into me   *(whole body)*
May light illuminate my spirit   *(head)*
And pour into my heart   *(heart)*
Thus will I find myself
Thus through power of the spirit
Will I be myself within me
Resting in God's wide world
                              (Quietness of soul)

Morning:

Mental image of the Rose Cross

May spirit light enliven my being's core.
                              (Quietness of soul)

Sunday, 9 a.m.: In the spirit of mankind I feel myself united
with all spiritual seekers.

Evening:

Meditation on the Rose Cross[32]

What this symbol shows to me
Is victory of life over power of death.
I will feel in me
The meaning of this symbol.
It will uplift me
And carry me uplifted
Into all spheres of life.

Morning:

In the beginning was the Word
And may the Word be in me;
And the Word was divine.
And with divine power
May the Word permeate me.
And the Word was a god
And may God bestow the Word
    upon my will.

During the day, the Subsidiary Exercises

Evening:

> *Review. Backwards. In pictures. 4–6 minutes*[33]
>
> *Mental image of the Rose Cross*
>
> > Upon the black cross
> > Bright rose stars
> > Image
> > In depths of my soul
> > Strong forces of spirit light
> > Reality
> > In me
> >
> > > *(Quietness of soul)*

Morning:

> Sunlight prevails throughout universal space
> Spirit light prevails throughout soul worlds
>
> > *(Quietness of soul)*

Six Subsidiary Exercises

Evening:

Review[34]

Oil

Bowl

Be for me a symbol
Of my I, which shines
In the flaming astral body
The flame lives on the oil
As my astral body lives
                in the etheric body

They rest within the body of senses
As does the oil in the bowl
                        (Quietness of soul)

Morning:

Mental image of the Rose Cross

Bright rose stars
On black wooden cross
Be for me the symbol
Of my soul
Strong forces of God's spirit
Shine in dark ground of soul
                Within me
                        (Quietness of soul)

Evening:

Review[35]

Meditating the Rose Cross

Before this picture
Place yourself, my I.
Seek within you the strength,
Seek within you the love,
Seek within you yourself.
Pledge that you will be strong
To the picture there before you.

Morning:

Meditating the Rose Cross

To the picture there before you
Pledge that you will be strong.
Seek within you yourself,
Seek within you the love,
Seek within you the strength,
Place yourself, my I,
Before this picture.

(Quietness of soul)

The Subsidiary Exercises

What is soul strength for me?[36]
What is life strength for me?
What is spirit light for me?

Down to the tips of one's toes

warm red background: *Love*
roses green: *Life*
cross white fluorescent light: *Knowledge*

As the roses of this ☩ *white/green*[37]
So the light of Christ
Out of the world's light.

As the roses of this ☩ *black/red*
So Christ's light
Out of the world's darkness.

Regarding the transformation of the colours of the cross from black into white and of the roses from red into green

The black cross with the red roses[38] depicts the development of the human being in the symbol of the profoundly significant Rosicrucian maxim.* The human individual experiences the symbol as a living element in which the spiritual forces live and weave, those forces which built him in the way he has been born out of the Godhead. He then comes to know that further development of his soul is made possible by applying his own strengths and forces. He knows that not only is his blood to become purified like the red plant juices of the roses but also that the black cross must be transformed when he purifies his enveloping nature and grows beyond what is merely personal in him by devoting himself to something immeasurably greater. He then dies into Christ, so that before his soul the dark, black cross is transformed into a shining, radiant cross. And the red roses expand to become an infinite circle when his soul enters more and more into the macrocosm, so that finally he feels himself to be that circle. In the all-embracing macrocosm the human being then experiences himself as being in a new existence.

Then, mysteriously, the colours of the symbol are transformed, so that the roses become green and the cross white.

---

* 'Ex Deo nascimur—In Christo morimur—Per Spiritum Sanctum reviviscimus.'

(handwritten: Mankind Comes from God / In Christ We die / Through the Spirit (Holy) We Are Revived / Resurrected)

The soul can only guess the full significance of this through sensing the power thus streaming towards it. The soul sees and recognizes this holy symbol as though shining towards it out of loftier spiritual spheres. Sternly and powerfully the symbol reveals itself to be a summons calling for continuous work towards the attainment of the great ideal which every human individual can realize once he is reborn in the Holy Spirit.

6. Rose Cross, Grail, Tao

However, those whose task it has been to bring the age-old wisdom forward right into our time then became interested in showing how the higher I of human beings, how the divine spirit of humanity which was born in Jesus of Nazareth through the event of Palestine, how that divine I has remained the same and been preserved in all those who have retained a proper understanding of it.[39]

As we described with regard to the individual in our comparison, namely that in his fortieth year he brought to birth his higher I, so did the writers of the Gospels describe the God in the human being up to the event of Palestine, namely how the God evolved, how he was reborn and so on. Those, however, whose task it was to show that they were the ones who carried forward from the writers of the Gospels, it was they who had to point out that this is now the time of the rebirth of the higher I, that one is concerned solely with the spiritual part which now outshines all else.

Those who called themselves the Christians of the John Gospel and whose symbol was the Rose Cross, they said: 'That which has been reborn for humanity as the mystery of the human being's higher I, this it is that has been preserved.' This is what was preserved by that closer community which originated in Rosicrucianism. Symbolically this continuity is indicated as follows. The vessel known as the 'Holy Grail', from which Christ Jesus had eaten and drunk with his disciples and into which Christ's blood had flowed and been caught by Joseph of Arimathea, this vessel, we are told, was brought to Europe by angels. A temple was built to house it and the Rosicrucians became the guardians of what was in that vessel, namely that which represented the being of the reborn God. The mystery of the reborn God held sway within humanity: the Grail Mystery.

This is the mystery which came to be represented as a new Gospel of which it is said: We look up to the wise man who wrote the John Gospel and who was able to say: 'In the beginning was the Word, and the Word was with God, and the Word was God.' That which was with God in the beginning is reborn in Him whom we saw suffering and dying on Golgotha, and who is risen. This continuity of the divine principle through all time, and the rebirth of this divine principle is what the writer of the John Gospel wished to portray.

All those who wished to portray this knew: that which was there in the beginning has been preserved. In the beginning was the mystery of the human being's higher I; in the Grail it is preserved, with the Grail it is united, and in the Grail there lives the I which is united with all that is eternal and immortal just as is the lower I with what is perishable and mortal. And those who are familiar with the mystery of the Holy Grail know that out of the wood from which the cross is made life springs forth, the immortal I which is symbolized by the roses on the black wood of the cross. Thus the mystery of the Rose Cross is something which can be seen as a continuation of the John Gospel. And with regard to the John Gospel and that of which it is the continuation we may quote the following words.

'In the beginning was the Word, and the Word was with God, and the Word was God. The same was in the beginning with God. All things were made by Him; and without Him was not any thing made that was made. In Him was life; and the life was the light of men. And the light shone in the darkness; and the darkness comprehended it not.'[40] Only a few individuals, who possessed something of what was not born of the flesh, comprehended the light which shone in the darkness. But then the light became flesh and dwelt among men in the figure of Jesus of Nazareth.

Thus in the terms of the spirit of the John Gospel one might well say: And that which lived as Christ in Jesus of Nazareth was the higher divine I of humanity as a whole, the reborn god become earthly in the likeness of Adam. This reborn human I continued as a holy mystery, was preserved in the symbol of the Rose Cross and is heralded today as the Rose Cross, the mystery of the Holy Grail.

That which can be born as the higher I in every human soul indicates to us the rebirth of the divine I in the evolution of humanity as a whole through the event of Palestine. Just as the higher I is born in every individual human being, so is the higher I of humanity as a whole, the divine I, born in Palestine; and it is preserved and further developed in that which is hidden behind the symbol of the Rose Cross.

And yet when we consider the evolution of the human being we find not only this great event, the rebirth of the higher I, but apart from this great event also a number of lesser ones. Before an individual can give birth to his higher I, before the soul can go through this great, all-embracing and incisive experience—the birth of the immortal I in the mortal setting—many profound prior stages have to be accomplished. Many and various preparations have to be made by the individual. When the great experience arrives he can say: 'Now I sense within myself, now I recognize within myself something which is looking down upon my ordinary I, just as my ordinary I looks down upon things in the sense world. Now I am the second within the first; now I have risen into those realms where I am united with the divine beings.' But when the individual has undergone this experience there are many further stages through which he will have to proceed, stages which differ from the preliminary ones, stages through which, however, he will be obliged to pass.

The ancient, secret sun oracles, whose wisdom was transplanted to the post-Atlantean cultures, were at work in the lands of Atlantis.[41] Two streams of humanity emanated from Atlantis. The one moved via Africa preparing the later Egyptian culture, and on to Asia, to India and the Orient as a whole, in preparation for the advent of the Light of Christ. The other moved via Europe to Asia, and portions of this stream of humanity settled in Central Europe. These peoples were directed by what came from the mystery centres which had the task of preparing the West to receive the Light of Christ when it came to them later. A sturdy race of human beings with powerful physical strengths was to be developed. Those mystery centres were to bring about valour, bravery and the forces of the heart. Lofty spiritual leaders from the heights of the spiritual world, unseen by human beings, guided those peoples and their mystery centres. One of these was King Arthur's

Round Table; others were the Druid shrines and the mystery centres of the Ingaevones. West Germanic culture group living along the North Sea

One great spiritual individual especially was at work during that period of preparation from the spiritual worlds focusing on Europe and its mystery centres. Titurel was his name. Titurel had as his servants the spiritual and worldly leaders of humanity, and it is only in this light that what they did is comprehensible. These facts are hinted at in myths and legends. The legend of the Holy Grail tells of the chalice filled with the blood of Golgotha being borne to Europe by angels. Titurel receives the chalice. He receives it as it hovers over European lands, and not until centuries have passed does he bring it down from the heights in order to found on the holy mountain (Montsalvat) the mystery centre of the Holy Grail. He could not do this until a number of individuals had become mature enough to receive the mystery of the Grail. Those ready for this initiation were each given the title of 'Parzival'.

Charlemagne, who came from the Orient—he was a reincarnation of a high Indian adept—was one instrument of that spiritual individuality symbolized by the title of Titurel. Flore and Blanchefleur, called Rose and Lily, are regarded spiritually as the parents of Charlemagne. They presided over this mystery.*

Through long meditations and concentration exercises, a 'Parzival' had cleansed his soul of all earthly wishes and selfish desires. He was a Cathar and as such he approached

ascetic

———————————

*Another note states: 'They presided over the mysteries into which Parzival later entered.'

King Titurel. By applying all the powers he had gained through long exercises he succeeded in bringing forth his higher I. He found himself face to face with himself. First he had to make the sacrifice of the intellect. And then he experienced what is laid down in the subsequent occult script.*

He saw his physical being as a symbol. And the whole physical world disappeared from his view. In its place he saw a huge, sprouting formation of plants and trees, as large as the whole earth. At the top of this he saw a great white lily growing up out of the tree of life. And a voice from behind him, the voice of Blanchefleur, said: 'This is you.' And he saw his soul cleansed of his urges and passions. Although the lily was splendid and perfectly formed it was surrounded by an atmospheric stench which pained Parzival. He learns that this aroma embodies everything he has discarded, has expelled in his catharsis. It now envelops him. He learns that he must take it all back again into himself, he must transform this painful stench of the lily. He must transform it into the pure, holy fragrance of the rose. And then the symbol vanished. It grew dark. And after a while Parzival was faced in the darkness by a second symbol: a black cross entwined with red roses. The tree of life had become transformed into the

---

* Another note states: 'He was a Cathar and stood, pious and pure, before his master Titurel. He told him that all the powers he had gained through his many years of meditation and concentration should now be applied in order to experience himself. First he had to make the sacrifice of the intellect. And as Parzival applied himself to using all the powers he had gained throughout his long years of exercises he succeeded in bringing forth his higher I. He found himself face to face with himself.'

black wood of the cross and the burgeoning fragrant roses
arising in him through the absolute dedication of the life of
the white lily to that tree. And the voice of Flore spoke behind
him: 'This you shall become.' The stench of the lily had
disappeared. The red roses had absorbed it. But Parzival saw
that this purification was still insufficient and that he must
nail his lower I to the black cross and imitate the life of Christ,
taking it into himself so that the red roses might come into
flower.

Hereupon Parzival departed into solitude where by day
and by night he caused these symbols to work upon him
inwardly. Little by little the symbols faded but the effect of
their force remained, now working in him like the force
which brings a seed to germination. In the depths of his
solitude he looked around him. He looked in front, he looked
behind, he looked up and down, he looked to the right and to
the left, and he sensed the mighty oneness of all things. And
he sensed the All-encompassing, the All-embracing One.
And he sensed how the All-embracing One sent his forces to
him from all sides, and he experienced himself as a point, as a
central point of all those forces.

He felt that point in his inner being to be a part of the great
All-embracing One. And then he felt a current flowing from

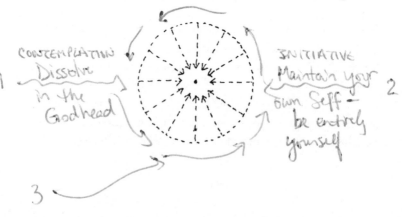

one direction, a current which flowed through him and urged him to dissolve entirely in this Godhead, in the forces of the All-embracing One. But from the other direction came another force, a force which would lead him towards maintaining his own self. And a third force joined these two, a force which brought it about that the two paths leading in opposite directions moved together in a circle.

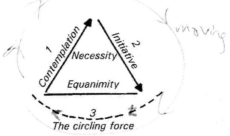

The circling force

1 is a force which enters into us, a force to which we must learn to devote ourselves entirely, a force which we also use, albeit unconsciously, when we concentrate our attention on an object. We must find this force through contemplation.

2 is a force which drives us to be entirely ourself, to maintain our selfhood; we also need it to maintain our enthusiasm, our initiative for our life in the external world.

3 is actually a circle, a force which comes from below, the circling force. This force drives us to see all the joyful and sorrowful experiences of life as being around us and not within us. We recognize in it the force which also works in the cosmos driving the stars to circle around us and which also works on us from out of the cosmos. Normally this circular line is drawn as a straight line. When we learn to comprehend this force we can regard with equanimity whatever life brings

us by way of joys and sorrows. We know that everything arises out of necessity; it is the driving law of karma.

Parzival has attained these three forces. He has surrendered himself to them. Thereupon from the left and from the right, like supports under each arm, came something resembling warm and cold wings. From the left he felt a supporting force under his arm streaming into his left side and generating warmth, spiritual fire; and from the right came a force which was cool, which made him feel cold. And then, in the region of his larynx, he felt currents coming from both sides. They came from the angels of light who bring the spiritual light of wisdom to human beings. He drew this spiritual light into himself. And then with the ears of the spirit he heard, tones resounding from the world of the harmony of the spheres, tones which made clear to him the purpose and destiny of the human being and of the world's becoming.

Again he waited for a while. And then something from above entered into his head, a sum of forces streaming down into him. Pouring into his whole being he experienced the force which, as the force of the Father, causes us to know the Creator in such a way that we feel ourselves to have been created by Him. And, as this experience endures, there grows above Parzival his own being in the form of a pentagram. He feels himself to be a son of this Father. And he experiences the truth of the Rosicrucian dictum:

E.D.N.—I.C.M.—P.S.S.R.[*]

All this was experienced by Parzival as he stood in solitude before Titurel.

---

[*] See footnote on p. 27.

We must be clear about the fact that Atlantis is the source of all wisdom of both East and West.[42]

Atlantis was a land enveloped in dense masses of watery mist. These dense masses of vapour had a quite specific relationship with the human being. They gave the human being of that time a certain sensation. They made his soul receptive for the language of the Godhead. In the rippling of the springs, in the rustling of the leaves the inhabitant of Atlantis heard the god speaking to him. And when he was alone and introverted within himself he heard a sound that was the voice of the god speaking to him. Thus he had no need of laws and commandments, for the god himself told him what he must do. That sound, which was heard all over Atlantis and which reverberated in the hearts of human beings in times of peaceful introspection, was later on in Egypt depicted in the Tao-sign: T. This is the original form of the cross.

Having reached an understanding of how those masses of watery mist enabled a connection with the divine to come about, so that the human being was able to have direct contact with and understanding of the wisdom of his god, let us now turn our attention to the water flowing through our landscapes. The sight of a dewdrop sparkling in the morning sunlight generates reverence in our heart. This shining dewdrop is like a memory of Atlantean times when water in the form of mist enveloped the land and the human being sensed the wisdom of the gods all around him.

The wisdom of Atlantis is embodied in water, in the dewdrop. Our German word *Tau*[*] is nothing other than the

---

[*] The German word for 'dew' is *Tau*.(Tr.)

ancient Atlantean sound when spoken. So let us regard with reverence and devotion every drop of dew sparkling on a blade of grass as a holy legacy from the time when the link between human beings and gods had not yet been broken. The sign of the Tao, the ancient sign of the cross, is known in Latin as *crux*. And what do we call dew, the dewdrop? *Ros*. 'Ros-Crux' is our Rose Cross.

This shows us its true meaning. It is the Tau or Tao of Atlantis, the wisdom of Atlantis, which shines out for us in the dewdrop. And the Rose Cross tells us exactly the same. It is a symbol for new life which will flower spiritually in the future.

7. The Rose Cross Meditation and the Rosicrucian Maxim

Out of the Godhead is the human being born.[43] Lofty
spiritual beings, cosmic forces, worked on his construction,
and thus he was built out of the cosmos, thus he grew forth
from the cosmos.

The first stage of evolution which hinted at the workings
of those cosmic forces was the one known to us as the
Saturn condition. That is where those forces began to work
in space and in time, so that Old Saturn came into being in
space and Old Saturn's evolution was accomplished in
time. There was back then no solar system with planets;
there was a body of warmth surrounded by the twelve signs
of the zodiac which poured their forces as though out of a
perimeter into that warmth body as their common focal
point. From that focal point other forces worked outwards,
but the counter-forces from outside were stronger, and that
is how the tendency for a centripetal development arose.
When one observes present-day minerals on our earth from
a spiritual perspective, one can detect the same effect but
now in connection with solid, earthly matter. Arriving from
all sides out of universal distances, spiritual forces work
inwards towards a common focal point in space, and in
that focal point a stone or a mineral arises. From that focal
point forces also emanate, but the inward working forces
are the stronger. Thus through the inward streaming of the
forces of the twelve constellations there arose the first

embodiment of the present-day earth as a globe of warmth, as Old Saturn.

Because the forces streaming inward towards the centre were dominant, a further degree of consolidation took place, together with a kind of fragmentation. As the evolution continued, further points formed in the central point, and thus in the end the whole planet consisted of many such points of force which had come into being through the working of the cosmic forces or the spiritual beings in the cosmos. Within those central points other spiritual beings were at work; they enlivened them and formed them in such a way that they became the potential beginning of what would later become human beings. That was when the human being received the forces which, as they continued to work, were able to give him the physical body in which today he lives as a self-aware earthly human. That was also when he was given the potential to form himself, through his own strength, into a spiritual human being. Back in those times on Old Saturn the seed was planted for physical life and for life in the spirit; the potential for a physical and a spiritual central point was created in the human being. When this development had reached a certain stage, the spiritual forces withdrew their working and a kind of planetary night, a state of rest, came about. And when the next day dawned the earth reappeared anew, now in its new embodiment as Old Sun.

Development continued. Building upon the Saturn stage which had gone before, everything was repeated under renewed conditions and a new stage emerged. The central points that had come into being on Old Saturn reappeared. Under the influence of the centripetal forces that were still at work, Old Sun became a more condensed heavenly body than Old Saturn had been. It became more compact and was also spatially less widespread. As a physical centre it did not need to send so many forces out into space. It was able to hold itself together more thoroughly and retain more of its own forces. This manifested in the way it was able to put up some resistance towards the influence of the zodiac, so that the light it sent out into its surroundings came from within it.

The consolidation of the physical aspect made it possible for something to be given off which worked spiritually. The same was also the case with regard to the various central points on Old Sun. They had the strength to radiate something of themselves, so that it became possible for their being to spread out into the surroundings, something one might describe as a growing in the light.

In the earthly development of our present time a similar force is at work in the plant kingdom, although now it is taking place within the solidity of earthly matter. Just as today's plants grow out of their seeds towards the light of the sun, so on Old Sun did a growing, a spreading out and an emerging into the light go forth from those central points into their surroundings. Not only on Old Sun did the forces of the twelve constellations work inwards from the environment, for Old Sun also confronted those forces with the light it sent forth from out of itself. Out of this there arose the potential for those planets with which we are familiar today in the new conditions of our physical solar system. Just as the diffraction of white light yields the seven colours, so, long ago, did the light of the sun itself provide the potential for the planets to arise as shining points of light.

or
old
Sun

Once again spiritual beings were at work in the central points, forming them into the potential for what in today's human being is the life body, or ether body. And the human being also received the potential for what he will one day create for himself as the life spirit. During the stage of Old Sun the principle of growth, of expansion, was developed both in the physical and in the spiritual central point of the human being. Just as the ether body provides the physical body with the power of growth, so does the life spirit signify that which will be revealed in the human being's environment as his spiritual central point.

The centripetal force at work in the stage of Old Saturn continued to work in the stage of Old Sun. Thus the process of condensation continued, transforming the globe of warmth into a globe of gas. The centrifugal force, on the other hand, enabled the sun to shine forth and at the same time caused the living creatures to emerge from their specific forms and grow.

After this development had been proceeding for some time a new lull occurred during which the cosmic forces withdrew their activity. And then the earth reappeared out of the world night in its new embodiment as Old Moon; and what had occurred during the two previous stages of development was repeated under new conditions. The consolidation, the concentration of the heavenly body and of the individual central points or bodies of living creatures continued, and this enabled the inner forces to become increasingly revealed. The centripetal and the centrifugal forces were both at work as they sought to become equal. This caused mighty vibrations. It manifested on the one hand in the centripetal forces causing a densification of Old Moon and in an ever-increasing separation of the central points from their surroundings. And on the other hand the centrifugal force expressed itself in the possibility of the spiritual forces of the central points becoming increasingly revealed in the environment.

These two forces worked in a way that led to a crisis in the development of Old Moon. The heavenly body underwent a kind of split. That part of Old Moon in which the centrifugal forces were especially influential split off from the other part, in which the centripetal forces continued to be especially active. One heavenly body thus arose which sent its forces outwards, revealing itself in the environment as the sun with its spiritual forces radiating outwards in the form of light; and another heavenly body arose as the moon which was prone to further consolidation and where the further development of those living beings took place which were subsequently to become earthly human beings.

This contraction caused the bodies of those creatures to become ever denser and ever more self-dependent, and the possibility also arose for a manifestation of stronger internal forces. As a result, whatever affected those living creatures from outside could continue to resonate within them, and they could also in a certain way react to them. A sound resounded from within them which was a repetition of the sound that approached them from their environment. Further consolidation had transformed Old Moon into a watery globe, and the bodies of the living creatures had also become more solid. Light from the sun continued to shine upon the moon, and those forces that were striving for spirituality and for greater refinement of matter were contained within this. The more refined part of Old Moon, which had separated itself out as a sun, was accompanied by spiritual forces, while the coarser part had been left behind. This spiritual element worked from the outside upon the part that was striving to become more dense, giving it light and life. As Old Moon, the coarser part revolved around that source of light. The same also applied to the various central points on Old Moon. When the division occurred, the part which was to become more spiritual while specifically developing the centrifugal force had accompanied the sun; and the part striving to become denser and develop the centripetal force remained with Old Moon while condensing to a watery state. The bodies of the living creatures were upon Old Moon; and the spiritual element which gave them life was outside those bodies, on the sun, whence it sent light into them.

There is something in the animal world as it manifests upon the earth today, something which corresponds to that effect, although it is now adapted to earthly conditions. The spiritual element that enlivens the physical bodies of the animals is not to be found within them. Outside the animal forms there is a spiritual central point from which life shines into them. On today's earth a whole animal species is enlivened by a single spiritual element. One can envisage that spiritual element as a central point giving life to the whole species which surrounds it.

In the same way Old Moon circled around its sun, the spiritual central point from which it received life. Because those spiritual forces had separated off from the moon and were working inwards from the outside while it circulated around the sun, movement came into being during the Old Moon period, and this also applied to the separate central points. Spiritual beings then formed these in such a way that they were able potentially to become what today's human being knows to be his astral body. Feelings and sensations stimulated by the external world are in constant movement within the human astral body. With these feelings and sensations he responds to that tone which approaches him from the external world.

During the Old Moon period the potential was also prepared for that member of the human being which would enable him to resound in spirit with the wisdom of the world and thus feel united with it. Just as the human being allows the stream of feelings to flow through his astral body, taking hold of it and then sending something to meet it, in order to react consciously, so does the light of world wisdom flow into his Spirit Self, and so does it become possible for him to take this light into himself and then consciously beam it back. Because Old Moon split into two heavenly bodies so that there were two heavenly bodies which influenced one another, movement arose and together with it conscious feeling and sensing. The influences went from one heavenly body to the other. The effects of the sun on the moon were felt to be forces coming from outside, and the same applied to the effects which went from the moon to the sun.

A conscious experience arose at the point where the sun forces encountered the moon forces. A kind of damming-up occurred where the inward-streaming force encountered the one coming out to meet it. For every living creature on the moon that was where the area of conscious experience ended; beyond this he was unable to manifest his forces because that was where his own outward-streaming forces came up against those streaming inwards. The living creatures which subsequently became human beings on earth did possess consciousness on Old Moon. But they did not possess self-consciousness for they were still entirely bound up with their environment. They had no experiences of their own; all they could do was allow what came to them from the outside world to reverberate within them.

When Old Moon had reached a certain degree of maturity, the spiritual powers who had brought all this about withdrew. The forces of sun and moon cancelled one another out; sun and moon gradually reunited and a period of rest ensued. And then the earth emerged out of that planetary night as a new heavenly body. Initially the former developments were repeated under new conditions. The earth underwent a period when its physical aspect was a body of warmth resembling that of Old Saturn. Then the various central points gradually re-formed under the influence of the centripetal force. Then came a period when the earth became a globe of gas as the centrifugal force made its influence felt as had been the case on Old Sun. The central points then began their emissions; that was the state of Old Sun on the earth.

After that came the repetition of Old Moon on the earth. The sun split off from the other part of the heavenly body, leaving behind the earth which still contained the moon forces. The forces which had departed with the sun were once again those which were striving for spirituality. From there they radiated light and life towards the heavenly body which was now beginning to regain its solidity. The sun was accompanied by the planets, so that only the moon forces remained united with the earth. As regards the various central points, in their case, too, those which were striving for spirituality had departed with the sun and thus rayed forth its force from there, whereas most had remained on the earth. A situation arose in which the conditions of Old Moon were repeated. The earth and the bodies of the living creatures became increasingly solid. The centripetal forces dominated.

But then a new phase began. In this new development of the earth, while the forces of the moon had remained, as had been the case on Old Moon, a new force, the actual earth force, had also arrived. This earth force was able to act as a uniting force between those of sun and moon, bringing about harmony and balance between them. As the process of solidification continued, because only the moon forces had remained united with the earth, the earth force created a kind of balance by separating itself from the moon forces. It left those forces behind on the moon, thus remaining separately between the impulses of both sun and moon, between those which strove for spirituality and those which strove for solidification. Both forces influence the earth; it contains both within itself but through its own strength it is able to maintain a balance between them.

The human being of today bears a similar force within his I. Just as the earth is the intermediary between the sun forces and the moon forces, so is the I of the human being the link between what is spiritual and what is material so that these two can unite within him. The earth, too, is situated in space in such a way that the moon with its rigidifying influence is all around it as is also the sun from which the light of the spirit streams towards it. The earth is as though enveloped by the forces of the moon while the forces of the sun stream towards it from a more distant central point far above the moon's enfolding shroud. The human I is enshrouded in a similar way, while the spiritual light also streams towards it from universal distances.   *like an "Earth" between Sun & Moon*

A third force had become active in the two forces which worked on one another during Old Moon. This third force was perpendicular to the other two. In the general realm of movement it brought about a new movement, what one might call the earth's own individual movement. The physical expression of this in the evolution of the earth is its rotation about an axis. On Old Moon the two forces generated a kind of stasis where they met. But now, through the encounter of those two with a third force, a double stasis came about which meant that general consciousness became limited and enclosed through having to become reliant upon itself. The intensification led to self-consciousness, thus sowing the seed of I-consciousness.

The same forces worked on the bodies of the living creatures with the result that each of those bodies became more self-reliant. Like the earth, they came to have their own capacity for movement, and this movement led to an even greater hardening. The bodies became more self-contained so that it was possible for each to have its own inner life. The further consolidation of the bodies was no longer caused solely by the moon forces but by the earth's own movement, its own forces, and those earthly forces were an aggregate of all that had gone before in the three earlier stages of evolution which had now been transformed into the fourth, the actual earth stage.

It was the spiritual beings who had created the possibility for the human being to become self-conscious by working during earthly evolution to prepare for I-consciousness, thus laying the foundation for his ability to refer to himself as 'I'. On earth the human being dwelt in the physical central point (or body), and under the guidance of the higher beings this gradually assumed the shape of the physical human body we know today. The inner force which formed the basis for I-consciousness could only come into being in a physical body which, in its independence, had to exist as a form that was separate from its environment. Gradually the physical human body did achieve this development, but prior to that the human being had already been given the predisposition for the I.

Just as Old Saturn's globe of warmth had condensed to form Old Sun's globe of gas after which it had been able to beam its own spiritual light out into space, and just as Old Moon's evolution had led to further solidification in the watery element and thus also to the revelation of more inward forces in sound and in movement, so in the earth's development did yet more solidification occur to form an earthly condition making possible a further revelation of inner forces which revealed themselves as life, as the individual inner life in the element of earth. On Old Saturn all was steeped in the dark ocean of warmth, on Old Sun everything shone forth as light, on Old Moon everything shuddered in sound, and now on the earth everything lives an inner life of its own.

Earth

Glow?

Fire
↓
Air
↓
Water
↓
Solid

When the repetition of the earlier planetary developments began, the earth was initially in a fiery state; the human being was living in the element of fire and his physical body also consisted of fire. During that period the main development was of the human being's will, and through his will he was able to influence that element. Even at that stage the tendency for I-consciousness had been prepared in him. Later, when he circled the earth in the element of air his body was in a gaseous state. And then there came a time of watery mist and his body was correspondingly within the element of water. He was mainly developing his feelings and through this he was able to influence the elements. At that time the human I still did not exist in the physical body. It existed outside the body while nevertheless having links with it. Not until the post-Atlantean era did the physical body densify to an earthly consistency, so that it then became possible for the human I to dwell within the physical body. And it was only then that the human being came to dwell properly on the earth. Through this he was able to develop the capacity of thinking and thus have an influence in the earthly realm.

Thus did the human being develop into what he is today. He was born out of the Godhead and is cocooned within the world's web, and all forces have worked to build him up from out of the great cosmos. The whole solar system was formed for his sake, and for his sake the four phases ran their course: as Old Saturn, Old Sun, Old Moon and now the earth itself. Countless beings have had to sacrifice themselves for him to enter into existence. We see some of these beings around us today, embodied in the lower earthly kingdoms; others we sense as forces at work within us. It was necessary for beings to exist who repeated the Saturn stage through all the three subsequent stages of the earth's evolution; and there were others who repeated the Sun stage and yet others the Moon stage so that now they are able to work and live in the mineral kingdom, the plant kingdom and the animal kingdom. There are also beings who work within the human being as though they had remained behind on Old Moon, on Old Sun and on Old Saturn.

The human being would be unable to live physically on the earth without the three lower kingdoms of nature, and he would be unable to develop his conscious I if he did not have these retarded forces within him. In his astral body he senses the working of beings who remained behind at the Moon stage as forces of hindrance which express themselves in urges and emotions of a lower kind also present in the animal kingdom. Beings of the Sun stage are at work in his ether body as inhibiting forces that bind him to habits and habitual ways of thinking. There is something plantlike in their effect. Just as the plant puts forth one leaf after another in constant repetition until something from the astral element intervenes by creating the flower, so do habits and adopted ways of thinking continually repeat until something new is brought about by the astral body through feelings and sensations. The beings who remained behind at the Saturn stage and are now at work within the human being pour their forces into his physical body as forces of hindrance, separating him from his environment with a feeling of being all on his own and having to stand up for himself. This engenders in him a sense of being his own personal central point, encouraging him to will, to think and to feel solely for himself while utilizing his environment for this purpose. This resembles the force that strives towards the central point in the mineral kingdom where the physical mineral is formed, for this force also generates a rigidity and an insularity which projects the human being back in upon himself. In the way these forces worked in the distant past upon Old Saturn, Old Sun and Old Moon they now work within the human being. He bears them within himself as inhibiting as well as encouraging forces, just as does the earth.

Since the time, in the post-Atlantean era, when the human being began to live on the earth in his physical body and with his I-consciousness, he has passed through several cultural epochs. And in each of these he has undergone a specific development. In the first, the Ancient Indian epoch, he worked especially on his ether body; in the second, the Ancient Persian epoch, he worked on his astral or sentient body; in the third, the Egyptian-Chaldean epoch, he worked on his sentient soul; and in the fourth, the Graeco-Latin epoch, he worked on his mind soul. During that fourth cultural epoch, when the human being had descended most deeply into matter, so that he was no longer able to perceive the spiritual world, something entirely out of the ordinary occurred, something which must be characterized as the greatest, most important event of earthly evolution. Golgotha

When the sun extricated itself from the earth and the moon it was accompanied by those forces which were striving towards the spiritual, and it then beamed back light and life into the earth. This involved something being removed from the earth which had initially been bound up with it. Without those forces—and especially as light and life were streaming back again—the earth was able to proceed to a certain point. And this was also the case for the beings living on the earth as human beings. They were able to develop an inner life up to a certain degree but they, too, had lost something spiritual through the departure of the sun. When the human being had developed in himself what was needed to be a human being on the earth, when, with the help of higher beings he had made of his physical body a temple for something divine and spiritual, then the God descended and dwelt in that temple. The spiritual forces of the sun then reunited themselves with the earth, and this made it possible for humanity to develop further in the spirit. Many divine spiritual beings had sacrificed themselves so that the human being could exist and develop; many cosmic forces had contributed to his creation.

But now the time had come when the greatest sacrifice would be made for humanity in that the highest spiritual being, God himself, who mirrored his spiritual life in the forces of the sun, descended to the earth in order there to dwell in a human body and pour his forces into the earth. The earth received the forces of the sun, and every living thing on the earth received the spirit. From having been a self-conscious earthly man, the human being was now able to arise as a self-conscious spiritual being. His mortal I became an immortal core that is alive in the spiritual light of the sun.

Something akin to what had taken place in the development of the earth now took place in the development of each individual human being and in humanity as a whole. After his physical birth the human being also undergoes the birth of his ether body and of his astral body; only then is he independent of his environment, only then can he develop his I further. He then forms his sentient soul, his mind soul in which the I especially comes to expression, and his consciousness soul in which the I rises above itself in order to develop the Spirit Self. At the very time when humanity is forming the mind soul during the Graeco-Roman cultural epoch, that member in which the I comes especially to expression, at that very time the I of humanity receives a new spiritual impulse through the fact that the God descends to earth and lives in the midst of humanity. That was when humanity became able to rise up to a higher spiritual life. Earthly humanity was able to rise above itself; it became possible for the I of humanity to develop into a divine I.

Just as the individual human being is first of all born in regard to his physical body, and then in regard to his ether body and his astral body, and just as only then can the I take effect within him, so was the earth initially born physically out of the cosmos as Old Saturn, and then etherically as Old Sun, and then astrally as Old Moon before reaching its earthly condition where the I could be developed. One can think of Old Saturn as the expression of the birth of the cosmic human being, of the macrocosm on the physical plane; of Old Sun as the period when the ether body was formed in the macro-cosm; of Old Moon as bringing about the astral body; and of the earth as the period when the mighty World-I was devel-oped. In the middle of that period of development the cosmic higher I descends from spiritual spheres and unites itself with the ongoing development of the earth. The spirit of the macrocosm descends into the World-I.

Thus is cosmic evolution mirrored in the human being, finding its expression in him. On the earth he is finally born out of the cosmos as a self-aware being. In his further evolution there is the possibility that he will learn to comprehend the spiritual impulse he has been given, so that he may be able to relive inwardly the example given by the World Spirit to humanity on earth.

Like a flower from the plant of humanity a human individuality opened itself to the spiritual sunlight long before those forces of the sun had reunited themselves with the earth. That individuality thus knew about the great event which awaited earthly evolution and about how it was to be furthered by an intermediary who, having come forth from humanity, would enter with his whole being into the sunlight so that it might fully take hold of him. He was to sacrifice his own being in order that in him the lofty Sun Being might reveal itself on earth. That individual bore this knowledge within his inner being. And when the time had come there grew out of humanity, like a living flower towards the sun, a human being. By sacrificing his three bodily sheaths to the Great Spirit, that human being was able to absorb into himself the spiritual sun forces so that the Great Spirit might come down and live within a human body on the earth. Just as the plant begins to die once fertilization has taken place, so was that body dedicated to the death forces once that event had taken place. When the blood from that body's wounds flowed upon Golgotha, the seed from the flower sowed itself in the earth as a new impulse for the spiritual life which was to grow further in humanity.

This impulse was laid into every human being as a spiritual seed so that it might continue to unfold when a human soul was stimulated by feelings and sensations to put forth a flower which might be fertilized by the spiritual light of the sun. The process that takes place spiritually in the soul is the same as that which comes about in the physical plant when the plant turns in upon itself, as though with a sense of shame, and begins to wilt. The human soul into which the light of the spirit has descended similarly feels profound shame at its own imperfection, and this feeling encourages it to go quietly into itself. Once a human being has sensed this spiritual light in his soul, it shines in upon him; and from this he learns to see himself for what he really is. So then he sets out along the path he is otherwise obliged to take when he departs from his bodily sheaths at death. He immerses himself into those sheaths and begins to die as an individual personality.

The human being dies as an individual personality and gradually finds himself living within the great World Being. He is thus able to say: 'In Christ I die.' With this new spiritual impulse he initially enters into his astral body. There he is met by the beings who work as those beings who have remained behind at the stage of Old Moon; they reveal themselves in all feelings, impulses and sensations of a more base nature. They stand at a stage below that of the developed I because they belong to the Moon stage. They are thus not permeated by the conscious forces of the I, for their nature is that of the animals. The human being there encounters whatever in the human astral body is at work by way of subconscious, unbridled feelings and sensations; he finds there a world which appears to him like an external environment. By confronting his own inner world in this way he gains the power to overcome those beings, to deliver them from his inner being and gradually to transform them.

The human being goes more deeply into himself when he enters his ether body. There he is confronted with a world which he has created through his way of thinking about whatever he has absorbed from his environment by way of traditions and habits. In his ether body, beings are at work who have remained behind at the Sun stage; they hinder his development as regards consciously free and independent thinking. Through the spiritual impulses he has received, these beings, too, will gradually be redeemed and transformed by him into wisdom-filled beings of light.

[handwritten margin note: we do the transforming now!]

Upon descending even further into his physical body, the human being will then find a whole world of forces working upon his will; these are beings who have remained behind at the Saturn stage. They harden his will with regard to the personal element which they guide more and more towards his personal central point. These beings, too, can be redeemed by him through the spiritual light which streams into his inner being out of a central point that lies outside his personality but with which he nonetheless feels intimately bound up.

In this way the human being initially experiences himself within his sheaths as the being he has thus far become. A new central point has arisen for him from which he can turn to look at himself. He knows that the three sheaths into which he has been obliged to descend are the result of earlier stages of the earth's development; and he knows that therefore he must find that strength in his soul which is to be especially developed during the earth stage and which has been prepared in his soul. This strength is what makes him a self-conscious I-being capable of becoming immersed in himself.

The plant seed gradually takes on the form of the plant and matures to attain an independent existence within that form. While his body remains alive, the human being steps through the portal of death by making himself independent of his bodily sheaths.

Then he finds within himself the spiritual seed which has been placed in his soul by the Christ Impulse. The Christ Light shines towards him, and just as the ripe seed falls into the earth once the plant has wilted, so does this spiritual seed fall out of his narrow personality and enter into the great light of the world. And then, from out of the depths of the earth, the light shines towards the human being, that light which has been united with the earth since the event on Golgotha. So then the human being can say to himself: 'In Christ I die, but I am reborn into a more all-encompassing existence.' And then he feels and experiences within himself the meaning of the words: 'He who loses his life for my sake, shall retain it.'

As the human being is born out of the macrocosm into the microcosm as a self-conscious I, so does he gradually return with his I-consciousness to live once again in the macrocosm. Having bestowed all their offerings upon him, the spiritual forces have gradually withdrawn from him so that he may now find his own way to the spiritual heights in order, in consciousness and freedom, to take up his abode in the spirit once more.

Initially the human being experiences those spiritual beings through his sense of intimacy with the great mother earth out of whom he has been born as an individual human being. Although he does still belong to her, that intimacy was far greater during the earlier stages of evolution. He experiences those stages as those of Old Saturn, Old Sun and Old Moon. He delves down into himself and experiences there those beings who are at work in his three sheaths, his astral body, his ether body and his physical body. Then he discovers his true central point, and the light of Christ streams towards him. He then also enters into the stages of earthly evolution where the three sheaths, the astral body, the ether body and the physical body of the earth were formed, and there he experiences the spiritual beings who are connected with that development and whose forces stream into it. The human soul then advances again and experiences that spiritual force which entered as the Light of Christ into the earth during its evolution.

This whole cosmic development with which the human being is interwoven presents itself as a mighty tableau. It plays out all around him; the whole development is interwoven with him. He sees himself as a focal point where the beings and forces active in this development meet. The forces stream into him and out again; he himself is the product of those forces. Among those forces he is to be found as a fixed centre, like an inner central point around which all this gathers; and that central point is the Christ Being, the centre of the macrocosmic and microcosmic evolution. As a new central point, from which everything flows and towards which everything flows, there shines towards him the source of all life, all evolution, as the divine spirit who stands behind all things and who was at work before any thing existed. Just as he feels himself, as an earthly human being, to be embedded in earthly evolution, so does he recognize himself as a spiritual being within that divine source of all life. The Christ Force lives in the depths of the soul, within the self-aware spiritual core of the power of the I. Beyond all bodily sheaths this force lives as the spirit-of-all-things, the Holy Spirit, as a higher I-force which is the true, eternal centre of all existence.

When the human being recognizes himself to be a spiritual being within this spirit-of-all-things he will be able to sense the significance of the words of the Rosicrucian maxim: 'In the Holy Spirit shall I be reborn.' He stands before his former self as a new being, a being who must now acquire the characteristics and skills he needs in this spiritual life, just as a child must learn to use his bodily limbs in the physical world. And this new spiritual being must experience within himself the three spiritual forces which are revealed in cosmic development as feeling, thinking and will, as love, wisdom and strength. Just as a child must first learn to stand and walk, so must the human being learn to find his direction and path in the spiritual world. This can only be acquired through the feeling of facing everything with love.

The human being must then learn to recognize the truth through understanding the world wisdom resounding within him with meanings he must learn to grasp, just as the child learns to understand speech and language. And then he gradually learns to recognize the true life of the spirit through experiencing himself to be in a central point from which his own impulses of will and of life emanate, so that he is thus able to reveal himself in his speaking and in his whole being. Hence the words of Jesus Christ: 'I am the way, the truth and the life. None shall come unto the Father except through me.' One cannot find the way to the true spiritual origin of existence, to the Father, if one has not developed these three forces in one's spirit and brought them together in the right way.

The development of the human being is illustrated in the symbol which belongs to the profoundly significant Rosicrucian maxim, the black cross with the red roses. The human being senses that there is something alive in this symbol, something in which the spiritual forces that have created him live and weave in the way he has come into being out of the Godhead. But then he also knows that further development of his soul is possible through the exertion of his own forces. Not only must his blood be purified like the red plant juices of the roses, but the black cross must also be transformed. He must purify his sheaths and rise above the merely personal when he devotes himself to something that is infinitely greater. He then dies in Christ, and before his soul the dark, black cross is transformed into a bright and shining cross. The red roses expand to form an infinite circle when his soul enters ever more readily into the macrocosm until the soul itself feels itself to be that circle. In the all-embracing macrocosm, the human being then experiences himself as having reached a new existence.

Then, mysteriously, the symbol's colours are transformed; the roses appear green, the cross white. The soul can only intuit the full meaning of this when it senses the power streaming towards it. The soul sees and recognizes this holy symbol shining towards it as though out of higher spiritual spheres. Sternly and forcefully it reveals its demand for steadfast work so that eventually the great ideal shall be attained, the ideal which every individual human being can realize when he is reborn in the Holy Spirit.

When we enter through meditation into an esoteric way of living we are obliged to reach a decision.[44] We must place something new at the centre of our life, something which has as yet not been a part of it but which must now become the main issue. The degree of success we have with our exercises will depend upon the intensity of that decision. One way of treating this esoteric life would be to take the exercises we are given as an addition to our everyday life, another job to be done like any other. But in that case we will notice that any progress made is not exactly outstanding. The decision should rather be to regard everything we encounter in ordinary life as being related to our esoteric life; to treat our esoteric life as the central aspect out of which we then direct all else and out of which something unceasingly flows into daily life.

What are we to achieve with our meditations? The intention is that by carrying them out in the right way we should develop great strength, a strength which is able to use the words of the meditation as a tool that will gradually enable us to create the spiritual organs in our astral body through which we shall be able to perceive our spiritual environment. The imprints we make in the substance of our astral body will only gradually become permanent. We might compare our astral body with an elastic mass which can indeed receive imprints before, after a while, regaining its previous form. We make these imprints during sleep, while the I and the astral body have departed from the physical and ether bodies. The more energetically and intensively we tackle our meditations, the more intensive do the imprints in the astral body grow until they become permanent and develop into organs which we call lotus flowers. This process is described in the saying given to us by the Masters of Wisdom and of the Harmony of Feelings:[*]

In the spirit there lay the seed of my body.
And the spirit incorporated into my body
The eyes of the senses,
That through them I might see
The light of the bodies.
And the spirit has imprinted into my body
Sensitivity and thinking
And feeling and will
That through these I might perceive the bodies
And work upon them.
In the spirit there lay the seed of my body.
In my body there lies the seed of the spirit.
And I will incorporate into my spirit
The supersensible eyes,
So that through them I might see the light of the spirits.
And I will imprint into my spirit
Wisdom and strength and love,

---

[*] With this designation, Rudolf Steiner was indicating highly developed individuals who are of the utmost importance for the evolution of humanity. 'These lofty beings have already travelled the road still faced by the rest of humanity. They now work as the great "Teachers of Wisdom and of the Harmony of Feelings for Humanity".' (From a letter of 2 January 1905, in GA 264, p. 86; see there also pp. 199–259.)

That through these the spirits might work upon me
And I shall become the self-aware tool
Of their deeds.
In my body there lies the seed of the spirit.[45]

However, we cannot properly make use of these organs until they have gained sufficient strength to enable them to imprint themselves from the astral body into the ether body. Not until the ether body has received that imprint will the portals open up for us before which stands the Cherub with the flame of the whirling sword.

We have heard that our physical and ether bodies could not survive for one second without the I and the astral body. Therefore, at the moment of falling asleep, when these two depart from the physical and the ether body, beings of a higher order enter into them, beings who in essence resemble our I and our astral body although they are of a much higher order. An Archangel takes the place of our astral body and a Spirit of Personality that of our I. We now encounter these higher spiritual beings if we have developed our astral organs; and this tremendous event, which is so sacred for us, is called by esotericists 'the encounter with the higher self'.

We should approach this moment with feelings of profoundest reverence and a sense of being utterly filled with its holiness. If we do not conduct our meditation with this attitude of genuine and unalloyed humility, the spiritual world will not reveal itself to us in its true form. Instead we will be confronted with all kinds of fantastic images, and the moral consequence for us will be a poisonous arrogance. If we are not sufficiently prepared by a genuine schooling for the world we seek to enter, it will be a blessing if the Cherub with the fiery sword stands in the way. The guardian of that paradise stands at the very point where we drift across when losing consciousness in deep sleep. If we did not lose consciousness this is where we would see him. A glimpse into the world of the Archangels would destroy us, for we would lack sufficient strength for such an encounter.

Why, then, is the Archangel who enters into our ether body termed our higher self? Why do we strive to become united with him? To answer this question we shall have to touch on a mystery connected with man's being. The human being visible to us here on the earth in his present state is actually a *maya*, he is incomplete. In ancient Lemurian times the earth had become so depopulated, so wasted that only one human pair remained upon it, a pair who had the strength to ensoul those animal-like entities. The other human beings had been distributed among the other planets. Thus present-day human beings are, basically, descended from that original pair. The biblical account of Adam and Eve is, also in this respect, quite correct, although clothed in an allegorical narrative.

It was Lucifer who then gained power over these first human beings, filling their astral bodies with his influences. Through these luciferic influences the ahrimanic influences also became accessible, and all of this made it possible for the human being to live his life in the physical, sense-perceptible world. As a result, the spiritual world became increasingly hidden behind physical matter which became for the human being an impenetrable covering. If the human being had continued to be solely influenced by the divine, spiritual beings who had created him, he would never have become free, although he would have remained capable of looking through matter and continuing to perceive the spirit.

Those guiding creative spirits then wanted to protect the ether body from also becoming entirely immersed in luciferic influences. They therefore separated off a part of Adam's ether body and retained it within the spiritual worlds. And it is this ether body[*] which is the higher self, with which we are to unite ourselves once more, for not until it is a part of us can we be complete human beings. It is up to the esoteric scholar to say to himself: 'Over there that higher element, which belongs to me, is waiting to be reunited with me; and in my meditations I must strive towards it with the utmost fervour, forming myself into a chalice which can contain that higher part.' Paul, who was an initiate in such matters, uses the correct expressions when he speaks of the 'old' and the 'new' Adam.[46]

The reuniting with a human being of that ether body which had remained behind took place for the first time when Jesus of Nazareth was born, as we are told in the Gospel of Luke. The Jesus Child there received Adam's ether body. With that part of Adam's ether body the lofty, guiding creative beings had retained for the human being the capacity of individual thinking and of an individual language. Of course the human being thinks, but it is not a kind of thinking which he himself produces individually, for he makes use of that divine substance of thinking with which the world is suffused. Similarly,

---

[*] In what follows 'ether body' always refers to that retained part of Adam's ether body.

the human being does not possess an individual language; lofty spiritual beings gave groups of human beings a common language. Individual human beings are to gain their own thinking and their own language through becoming reunited with their higher ether body. The fact that the capacity for language is contained in this ether body explains the meaning of the legend which tells of how the Jesus Child did not need to learn a language, for when he was born he spoke with his mother in a language she understood.

Through once again uniting itself with a physical human body, Adam's ether body became subject to the law which applies to all spirituality when it descends into matter, the law of number, of replication. Just as the seed placed in the earth brings forth the ear containing many grains, so did the body of Jesus become the earthly womb for the ether body of Adam, the point of entry for replication, and those replicated ether bodies are now ready and waiting for us. When we are rapt in our meditation, when our whole external life disappears and we hear and see nothing, we shall come to feel as though we are dying away in order, through becoming united with our higher self, to be revived again.

That is why, for the more recent, rightfully existing esoteric schools, the cross is the symbol of resurrection to new life. It is not a birth that is seen as the starting point of this life; it is a death, the death of Christ upon the cross of Golgotha; and this life is symbolized by the sacred blood flowing away. That is why, in the Rose Cross, we have the dead plant substance, the desiccated wood, with the living red roses sprouting from it. We are to gain the feeling in our meditation that we are born out of God—just as we are told in our principal maxim, which is intended to be the maxim of our esoteric life—and that we die in Christ through causing the power of our meditation to light up within us and shine out into the higher worlds; and our higher self comes towards this warmth, towards this light, uniting itself in this way with us as the Holy Spirit in whom we come alive again:

Ex Deo nascimur Out of God we are born
In Christo morimur In Christ we die
Per Spiritum Sanctum reviviscimus. By the Holy Spirit we are resurrected.

Our souls must bow down before that which has been prepared in the culture of Central Europe, especially in the way it expresses how we stand between two forces that swing back and forth through the world, two forces between which it is up to us to find the balance.[47] We must fully understand that on the one hand the world is striving towards ahrimanic rigidity, towards becoming ossified in the fire of materialism, while on the other it is aspiring to rise up egoistically into something abstractly spiritual. To proceed in either the one direction or the other would lead to the utter ruin of Central European humanity.

To follow a science bound up entirely with external sense perceptions would lead us to tear the roses off the cross and become fixated solely on what has become rigidified. We would gradually arrive at a view of the world that would turn us entirely away from anything spiritual; we would see nothing but what has become ahrimanically rigid. Try to imagine the ideals of ahrimanic science. It is a world of whirling atoms, an entirely materialistic view; it is a view of the world from which everything spiritual must be banished.

People like to think—and they even teach it to children in school—that once upon a time there existed a whirling gaseous mass out of which the sun came into existence and which then also ejected the planets. One demonstrates this to children in school by putting a drop of oil into a bowl of water. A circular bit of paper with a pin through it is placed on the drop. The pin is rotated and this causes droplets to spin off, creating a miniature planetary system. The desired proof is evident, but the most important fact is forgotten: the teacher has to spin the pin. So, if one wants to enter into this in all honesty, one is in truth obliged to imagine 'the great schoolmaster' out there in space twiddling away with the pin.

Thoughts and feelings that tend in the direction of Ahriman do indeed lead one to imagine the sun and the planets coming into existence in this way. And this in turn led to a historical concept once described by Herman Grimm thus: A rotting bone with a hungry dog circling round it is a more appetizing image than this view of the world based entirely on that Copernican view.

This is the one danger, to tear the roses from the cross, leaving nothing behind but the black, charred cross. The other danger is to tear the cross from the roses and strive solely for the spirit while despising what the Godhead has placed into world evolution, instead of entering lovingly into the idea that whatever exists here in the sense-perceptible world is an expression of the divine. This is the one-sided, religious view despised by science, the view that unconsciously tends towards the luciferic element from the East, just as science, which wants to tear the roses from the cross and retain only the charred cross, strives towards the West.

We here in Central Europe, however, are called upon to retain the roses on the cross and what is expressed by linking the roses with the cross. When we contemplate the rigid cross, we sense that whatever is rigidly physical in the world has departed from the divine realms and entered into the world. It is as though spirituality has created for itself an environment in matter: *Ex Deo nascimur.*

When we comprehend the matter correctly, we also sense that we should not enter into the spiritual world only in the company of Lucifer but rather that we die by uniting ourselves with that which has descended into the world out of the divine higher self: *In Christo morimur.*

And by combining the cross with the roses, the materialistic world-view with the spiritual world view, we sense how the human soul can awaken in the spirit: *Per Spiritum Sanctum reviviscimus.*

That is why the cross entwined with roses was the symbol for one who entered profoundly into the culture of Central Europe: Goethe. And that is why it must be our symbol too. So let us, [...] in so far as we are able to be present here in the future, remember what must be our ideal aim in view of the great tasks facing earthly evolution: to entwine the cross with the roses, neither to tear the roses from the cross so as to retain hold only of the cross, nor to cherish only the roses while rushing with them into the spiritual flowering of abstraction.

Notes

1. Notes of a lecture to members, Leipzig, 15 December 1906 (GA 97, pp. 84f.).

2. From Goethe's poem 'Selige Sehnsucht' in *Divan of West and East*.

3. John 1:5.

4. Lecture to members, Cologne, 25 December 1907 (GA 98, pp. 64–7).

5. The first few lines of Goethe's fragmentary epos *The Mysteries*, translator unknown.

6. Lecture to members, Cologne, 25 December 1907 (GA 98, pp. 76–8).

7. Lecture to members, Stuttgart, 16 September 1907 (GA 101, pp. 182–92).

8. Public lecture, Berlin, 14 March 1907 (GA 55, pp. 176–82).

9. Johann Wolfgang Goethe, *Faust Part I*, Night (Tr. David Luke).

10. Ibid.

11. Public lecture, Berlin, 14 March 1907 (GA 55, pp. 183–206).

12. Johann Wolfgang Goethe, *Faust Part II*, in the final verses (Tr. David Luke).

13. Johann Wolfgang Goethe, *Faust Part I*, Night (Tr. David Luke).

14. From Goethe's fragmentary epos *The Mysteries*.

15. Lecture to members, Cologne, 29 December 1907 (GA 101, pp. 250–6).

16. Public lecture, Berlin, 10 February 1910 (GA 59, pp. 91–8).

17. Answers to questions, Dornach, 26 August 1921 (GA 77b, p. 105).

18. GA 13, pp. 307–16.
19. Ibid., pp. 359–62.
20. Lecture to members, Leipzig, 21 November 1910 (GA 125, pp. 185–8).
21. Public lecture, Berlin, 15 December 1910 (GA 60, pp. 200–6).
22. Esoteric Lesson, Kassel, 26 February 1909 (GA 266/1, pp. 449–52).
23. This meditation is included, *inter alia*, in GA 266/2, p. 21.
24. Esoteric Lesson, Hamburg, 14 March 1909, Notes A and B (GA 226/1, pp. 465–8).
25. Lecture to members, Vienna, 28 March 1910 (GA 119, pp. 202–13 and pp. 214–15).
26. Archive No. A 0066 (GA 267, p. 254).
27. Archive No. A 0104 (ibid., p. 307).
28. Archive No. A 0023 (ibid., p. 308).
29. 1910 or later, Archive No. 7104 (ibid., p. 334).
30. 1910 or later, Archive No. A 0114, originally in English (ibid., p. 337).
31. 1912, Archive No. 3231 (ibid., p. 338).
32. April 1912 or May/June 1913, Archive No. A 0033 (ibid., p. 344).
33. 9 November 1913, Archive No. A 6630 (ibid., p. 373).
34. *c.* 1913, Archive No. A 0100 (ibid., p. 376).
35. November 1921, Archive No. A 0021 (ibid., p. 392).
36. Archive No. 4422 (ibid., p. 422).
37. Archive No. 3193 (ibid., p. 423).
38. Ibid, p. 480.
39. Lecture to members, Kassel, 24 June 1909 (GA 112, pp. 18–21).
40. John 1:1–5.

41. Esoteric Lesson, Munich, 27 August 1909, Note B (GA 266/1, pp. 506–11).

42. Esoteric Lesson, Munich, 1 June 1907, Note A (GA 266/1, pp. 218f).

43. Regarding the Rosicrucian maxim: presumably this was written down by Rudolf Steiner, but no original is extant. The text here is taken from a handwritten record with an annotation 'F.M.' (GA 265, pp. 250–69).

44. Esoteric Lesson, Munich, 7 December 1909 (GA 266/1, pp. 546–50).

45. The verse is amended in accordance with GA 266/1, p. 89.

46. 1 Corinthians, 15:45f.

47. Lecture to members, Prague, 15 May 1915 (GA 159, pp. 260–3).

Sources

The following volumes are cited in this book. Where relevant, published editions of equivalent English translations are given below the German titles.

The works of Rudolf Steiner are listed with the volume numbers of the complete works in German, the *Gesamtausgabe* (GA), as published by Rudolf Steiner Verlag, Dornach, Switzerland.

RSP = Rudolf Steiner Press, UK
AP / SB = Anthroposophic Press / SteinerBooks, USA

GA

3   *Wahrheit und Wissenschaft* (2012)
        Truth and Science (Mercury Press)

10   *Wie erlangt man Erkenntnisse der höheren Welten?* (1993)
        Knowledge of the Higher Worlds (RSP) / *How to Know Higher Worlds* (SB)

13   *Die Geheimwissenschaft im Umriss* (1989)
        Occult Science (RSP) / *An Outline of Esoteric Science* (SB)

55   *Die Erkenntnis des Übersinnlichen in unserer Zeit und deren Bedeutung für das heutige Leben* (1983)
        Supersensible Knowledge (AP)

57   *Wo und wie findet man den Geist?* (1984)

58   *Metamorphosen des Seelenlebens—Pfade der Seelenerlebnisse. Erster Teil* (1984)
        Transforming the Soul, Vol. 1 (RSP)

From the History and Contents of the First Section of the Esoteric School 1904–1914 (AP)

265   *Zur Geschichte und aus den Inhalten der erkenntniskultischen Abteilung der Esoterischen Schule 1904–1914* (1987)
'Freemasonry' and Ritual Work, The Misraim Service (SB)

266/1 *Aus den Inhalten der esoterischen Stunden. Gedächtnisaufzeichnungen von Teilnehmern. Band I: 1904–1909* (2007)
From the Esoteric School, Esoteric Lessons, Volume 1: 1904–1909 (SB)

266/2 *Aus den Inhalten der esoterischen Stunden. Gedächtnisaufzeichnungen von Teilnehmern. Band 2: 1910–1912* (2007)
From the Esoteric School, Esoteric Lessons, Volume 2: 1910–1912 (SB)

267   *Seelenübungen Band I. Übungen mit Wort- und Sinnbild-Meditationen zur methodischen Entwicklung höherer Erkenntniskräfte, 1904–1924* (2001)
Soul Exercises, Word and Symbol Meditations, 1904–1924 (SB)

284   *Bilder okkulter Siegel und Säulen. Der Münchner Kongress Pfingsten 1907 und seine Auswirkungen* (1993)
Rosicrucianism Renewed, The Unity of Art, Science and Religion. The Theosophical Congress of Whitsun 1907 (SB)

All English-language titles are available via Rudolf Steiner Press, UK (www.rudolfsteinerpress.com) or SteinerBooks, USA (www.steinerbooks.org)